W9-CPO-364

362.4   51167
Bow

Bowe
Comeback

WITHDRAWN

H S LIBRARY - BAYTOWN, TX.

COMEBACK

Other Books by Frank Bowe

1817

HARPER & ROW, PUBLISHERS, New York
Cambridge, Philadelphia, San Francisco,
London, Mexico City, São Paulo, Sydney

362.4
Bow

COMEBACK

Six Remarkable People Who Triumphed Over Disability

FRANK BOWE

Foreword by William Glasser, M.D.,
Author of *Reality Therapy:
A New Approach to Psychiatry*

51167

WITHDRAWN

LEE H. S. LIBRARY - BAYTOWN, TX.
3291

COMEBACK. Copyright © 1981 by Frank Bowe. All rights reserved. Printed in the United States of America. No part of this book may be used or reproduced in any manner whatsoever without written permission except in the case of brief quotations embodied in critical articles and reviews. For information address Harper & Row, Publishers, Inc., 10 East 53rd Street, New York, N.Y. 10022. Published simultaneously in Canada by Fitzhenry & Whiteside Limited, Toronto.

FIRST EDITION

Designer: Robin Malkin

Library of Congress Cataloging in Publication Data

Bowe, Frank.
  Comeback.

  Bibliography: p.
  1. Physically handicapped—United States—Biography.
I. Title.
RD796.A2B68   1981   362.4′092′2 [B]   80–8195
ISBN 0–06–010489–9   AACR2

---

81 82 83 84 85 10 9 8 7 6 5 4 3 2 1

FOR WHITNEY, WITH ALL MY LOVE

3/82 B&T 8.50

CONTENTS

FOREWORD

There are two kinds of disabled people, those who disable themselves by believing they cannot cope with what they perceive is a harsh world and those who are physically or mentally handicapped so that, harsh world or not, they are physically less able to cope. In my work as a reality therapist I deal mostly with the first group, those who, in a sense, have chosen to handicap themselves. What I do is to teach them that they have the resources to cope if they will stop fearing they can't and start learning how. For them the handicap is much more in their head than in the reality they face.

Frank Bowe, on the other hand, writes of people who through their success in overcoming crippling physical disabilities vividly demonstrate to all of us, handicapped or not, that to succeed the world is less the problem than ourselves. Here are six people, ranging from a blind woman who battles for the rights of all handicapped people to a brilliant physicist refusing to give up even though he suffers from ALS or "Lou Gehrig's disease," who do not accept that their limitations are defined by their handicap. They have taken charge of their own lives and accomplished far more than seems possible to most of us. The key to what they have been able to do lies in the knowledge that they have somehow learned, what so few of us seem to learn, which is that we are biologically constructed to control our own destiny and that all of our behavior, good, bad, and miserable is to do just this. Knowing this they do not waste their time and effort choosing misery and self-pity. They recognize much more clearly than we do that what they do is their choice and that, given any situation, they have many more choices than to give up and settle for defeat.

Their badly damaged bodies seem to have led them to see that their only course is not to blame the world but to try to control it so they can succeed in it. The lesson here for all of us (in fact, maybe more for the nonhandicapped than for the handicapped people who may read this book) is that those who take their health for granted tend to blame the world rather than look to themselves when they find reality hard to deal with. In this book it is made abundantly clear that it is not the world that is at fault. I do not deny that the world may seem overwhelming for all of us at times, and that it is not easy to be poor, old, sick, or lonely. But the worst handicap of all is to believe that nothing can be done except to choose to suffer as our best attempt to change a grim situation that we may find ourselves in.

Read this book and then look at your life. Ask yourself whether you want to continue to accept the limits you believe that the world sets for you or whether you want to stop complaining and start taking charge of your life and dealing with the world more effectively. Consider how many more tools you may have to do so than the remarkable people of this book.

> William Glasser, M.D.
> Author of *Reality Therapy;*
> *A New Approach to Psychiatry*

PREFACE

IN *COMEBACK,* I have drawn profiles of six people who have fascinated me. All faced severe disability early in life. Each surmounted the many complex problems associated with disability to achieve independence as a self-sufficient citizen. To do so represents a triumph of will over adversity, of determination over long odds, and of mind over matter. These three men and three women have triumphed over the most devastating of impairments—paralysis, mental retardation, loss of vision, childhood polio, loss of hearing, and deaf-blindness. It is in this sense that they have "come back."

Yet if this were all they had done, it is doubtful I would have chosen to write about them. I have been fortunate to have come to know many hundreds and even thousands of people in this country and throughout the world who have overcome disability. The six people in this book have done much more.

Our views of the universe we inhabit have been altered forever by the work of Stephen Hawking, the Cambridge University theoretical physicist who has taken his field further than anyone since Albert Einstein. No one familiar with Hawking's work can ever again look at the star-filled skies in quite the same way. Our understanding of the complex mysteries of human intelligence is being changed by the work of Nansie Sharpless and her colleagues as they investigate the chemistry of the brain. Sharpless, a neurochemist at the Albert Einstein College of Medicine in The Bronx, New York, is studying what are called "neurotransmitters," substances believed to be the messengers of the brain. Anyone interested in human sexuality will find his beliefs challenged by the hotly controversial work of Susan Daniels at Louisiana State University's medical center. As a researcher and as a teacher, Daniels is redefining the very meaning of the word sexuality.

Then, too, people interested in the decades-old battle between those who believe heredity determines our fates and those who champion the role of the environment will discover intriguing new ideas in the life of Roger Meyers. Meyers's determination to control his own fate frankly awes me. The poetry of Robert Smithdas stands as a glistening gift to all of us, awakening slumbering feelings and sharpening vague perceptions. Smithdas is the only deaf-blind person ever to go further in education and in work than the famous Helen Keller. And few people interested in politics can fail to learn from and be inspired by the example of Eunice Fiorito. She has caused something of a sea change in our national political climate by mobilizing a previously quiescent minority into a powerful presence in Washington.

These are not inconsiderable achievements. They represent accomplishments beyond those of most people, disabled or not. To my own mind, these are perhaps the most important contributions one can make to his country and to the world: this is a different place, and a better one, because these people lived.

It is a delightful irony for me that the three men and three women in this book do not see their lives in quite such exalted terms. Again and again, as we met and talked, they would say: "I'm not sure how I could have done it any other way" or "I didn't do much of anything; I just kept going."

Physics, neurochemistry, sexuality, psychology, poetry, and

politics: the range of fields in which these people have made contributions suggests that they are a motley lot. And that is true: I have found them to be a strikingly diverse group. It is part of their fascination for me that they have dealt with their lives in such unique ways. If any proof was needed that there is no one "right" way to cope with disability, these profiles offer compelling evidence.

These people are special to me in yet another way. They illustrate for me one fact I have found searingly important for the United Nations International Year of Disabled Persons (1981): people with disabilities are people with abilities. That there are in this world one-half billion such people never ceases to amaze me. Six out of every ten of these are not receiving even the most rudimentary special education, rehabilitation, or job placement services they need and deserve—largely because few people appreciate the abilities that are there, camouflaged and submerged, no doubt, by very visible disability.

The United Nations proclaimed two dominant themes for the Year: "full participation" and "equality." The first speaks to the need to integrate people with disabilities into the full range of life in communities, regions, and nations. The second stands for the ideal of fair treatment under law. Both are critical if people with disabilities are to have an opportunity to live the kinds of lives they potentially can lead. The absence of either often suffocates the drive and spirit that help disabled people rise above disability and test their abilities to the furthest limits they can perceive.

These are goals embraced in the United States by the American Coalition of Citizens With Disabilities (ACCD), the organization I headed during the period in which I came to know these six people. Because most of them related to me at least in part in my role as ACCD's director, a brief word about the coalition and its work may help the reader.

Founded in 1974 by a group of disabled leaders from across

the nation, ACCD is dedicated to advancing the human and civil rights of people with mental, physical, sensory, and emotional impairments. ACCD believes that there are as many as 36 million disabled Americans. The organization does not provide individual counseling or training, but rather focuses upon broad social-policy goals, particularly as expressed in legislation and regulations.

I have often described the work of ACCD's director by saying that I saw the role as ensuring that when a person with a disability arrived at a gaming table, as it were, the deck would not be stacked and the dice would not be loaded. In other words, the coalition strives to make the rules of the game fair. What disabled people do from there, how well or poorly they fare at the game, is entirely up to them. ACCD's role ends when the game begins.

The game has been grossly unfair for disabled people throughout history. Of the estimated 500 million such persons in the world, fewer than 300 million are even given basic life-support services. Fewer than one in ten is now protected in any significant way from unjust discrimination.

That is true of the six people in this book: they grew up, got an education, and secured employment despite the virtual absence of any statutory rights shielding them from the oppressive effects of discrimination. Rather, through personal perseverance and assistance from family and friends, they won despite lopsided odds. Their victories helped show the way for others and played a central role in convincing lawmakers and bureaucrats in the United States and in other nations that disabled people deserve protection under law.

Despite recent progress, I expect it will be many years before most disabled people are given an equal opportunity to live, grow, and support themselves. So the conditions that these people faced are in many respects typical of those hundreds of millions of disabled people confront today and will encounter tomorrow. What is not typical is the way these people responded: they ripped through the barriers of prejudice and made their own marks upon the world.

It was in this context, then, as ACCD was trying to shape the rules of the game, that these six remarkable people came to my attention. They have helped shape my own thinking, expand my horizons, and enrich my appreciation for what is most essentially human about human beings. Although each in his or her own way helped me in my work at ACCD, and I have tried to help them in some small way, they have given me far more than I can ever realize or thank them for.

It is my hope that you the reader will come away from these brief portraits with a sense of knowing not only six fascinating people, but also one other remarkable individual: yourself. Someday, somehow (the chances are better than one in four), disability will touch you or someone close to you. Having had the chance to meet these people may, I hope, help you in responding to that challenge.

And even if you and those you know never experience disability, I hope you will find in these people something to spark within you a sense of wonder at just what the human being is capable of doing.

It is the abilities, not the disabilities, that count. It is upon these strengths, talents, and gifts that our futures rest. If there is anything I have learned in my work with disabled people around the world, it is that they are capable of much more than we have ever dreamed.

COMEBACK

1

EUNICE FIORITO

"I am a human being who happens to be blind, not a blind being who happens to be human."

EUNICE FIORITO, five feet nine inches and 180 pounds of in-domitable will topped by a shock of blazing red hair, is a force to be reckoned with in American politics. She can be warm and ebullient, inspiring great loyalty, confidence, and dedication. She could also be a hellion inciting a crowd to riot, a politician so adept at maneuvering people to get what she wanted that even so skilled a Washington hand as Joseph Califano shied away from confronting her.

Almost single-handedly, Eunice has pulled together America's largest minority, the 36-million-strong disabled population, given them a united voice in an organization she helped found and served as its first president, and kept them working together on issue after issue. She convinced highly skeptical leaders of the different groups of disabled people that her vision of a united front would in fact work—and she labored hard to make sure it did.

Because Eunice never relented in her pursuit of equality of opportunity for disabled people, these people today have rights they never before enjoyed, anywhere in the world. They have services they need, better equipment and more devices; but most of all, they have a chance.

Eunice never forgot that her first job paid her five cents an hour—alongside other blind people, some with college degrees, earning no more than ten cents an hour. She never forgave those who denied her, and others with disabilities, the opportunity to design their own lives and determine their own fates. In the face of such oppression and discrimination, Eunice believed that bold aggression was not only appropriate, it was required. "I have been described as a manipulator and that is a fact," she told me, her candor disarming. It was a creative manipulation, not a harmful one, designed to produce a reality that matched her vision of a better world.

She has often been described as the disability rights movement's answer to Bella Abzug, the "Battlin' Bella" with the wide-brimmed hats who represented Manhattan in the U.S. Congress for some years and whom Jimmy Carter fired as chairperson of a women's advisory group for being too aggressive. It is not a comparison that bothers Eunice. "I see myself as a very forceful person. I am an actress. I use my relationships, consciously giving people different impressions. I have been described as aggressive, but I prefer the term assertive. I call a spade a spade, and I probably don't have the kind of tact one needs to have. Being firm and direct is how I get things done."

When she has to, Eunice can be uncompromisingly aggressive. When the Ford administration delayed carrying out a 1973 law protecting the rights of disabled people in federally sponsored programs and activities, she brought to bear all the pressure she knew how to force action. Finally, after three years of inexcusable procrastination, Eunice felt the time had come for confrontation politics. By law and presidential decree, Health, Education, and Welfare Secretary David Mathews was the one individual who could end the delay. Eunice flew to Washington, meeting that evening with Mathews's chief civil rights aide Martin Gerry and demanding a meeting with the secretary the following morning. She got it.

Telling me about the meeting later with obvious relish, Eunice re-created the scene in the secretary's office. "All of a sudden, a hand popped on my head. This southern voice said, 'Isn't it good to see you again? We have met.' Well, I don't like to be treated like a puppy dog and patted on the head, so I decided not to give him the courtesy of standing up. 'Mr. Secretary,' I said, 'perhaps we ought to do this in a professional manner. I don't recall having the pleasure of meeting you, but obviously you have the advantage of having seen me.' He sat down and started speaking to me in a totally condescending manner, in complete command of the situation. I interrupted him after fifteen minutes of this. 'Mr. Secretary, now that you have talked to me in this fashion, you deserve to be talked to in the same way.' The room fell silent; everyone was horrified at the way I was treating this cabinet officer. I didn't care. I went nose-to-nose. I stuck my face in that man's face and I tore into him.

"I told him that if he didn't come forth with a plan to protect these rights, I had a plan for him—and he wouldn't like it. 'We'll hold a demonstration at the Republican National Convention this summer, Mr. Secretary, but you know we won't make trouble. All of us will wear black. People in wheelchairs will push coffins draped in black around the convention center in Kansas City. And when the press comes, why, we'll tell them that Mr. Ford and you are in favor of killing off disabled people, that we know Ford's reelection would mean we would be dead soon, and so this is a mourning.' Mr. Mathews understood what that would do to the Republicans' chances in November. So he said, 'Let's talk,' and we made a deal: the secretary would enforce the law and I would call off the demonstration."

The plan was for proposed regulations outlining how the law, section 504 of the 1973 Rehabilitation Act, would be implemented, to be published immediately. Nationwide hearings and an extended public comment period would follow. Mathews promised to publish the final regulation, which would have the force of law, before the election in November.

He kept the first part of his promise, but not the second. By that time, I had assumed my duties as ACCD's director. At Eunice's behest, I met with Mathews in the final days of the Ford administration but failed to get him to issue the regulation in final form. When Jimmy Carter took office, Eunice and I met with Mathews's successor, Joseph Califano. He promised to review the work done to date and to promulgate final regulations shortly. But by this time, Eunice's patience was at an end. She wanted those rules out, and she wanted them enforced immediately.

At the ACCD board meeting in Denver in March of 1977,

Eunice led the board to adopt a nationwide demonstration program I had suggested. It called for a sit-in in each of HEW's ten regional city offices. ACCD sent a letter to Carter, with a copy to Califano, announcing its intention to act if the final rule was not published by April 4, 1977. It was not, so we proceeded with the plan.

Eunice herself led the critical sit-in in the Washington headquarters of HEW. She raised the crowd of several hundred disabled demonstrators to a fever pitch of excitement, singing "We Shall Overcome" and other protest songs. When Califano entered the room, Eunice stood on a pedestal in the midst of the demonstrators, loudly challenging him to come to her. The secretary looked about in confusion, turned to his aides, and declined. He knew he could not win if he played by her rules. Instead, he stood at the opposite end of the room and promised publication of the regulation by May. Eunice rejected the compromise, and the sit-in was on.

Califano and his lieutenants tried every trick they knew to stop the protest. They cut off all communication from the demonstrators to the outside world, cordoned off the building, refused to permit food and medical supplies to be admitted, and tried to divide the demonstrators against themselves by sowing discontent in their ranks. Eunice even had to negotiate the following morning, after an all-night sit-in, for coffee and doughnuts. She urged demonstrators all over the country to keep up the vigil. The San Francisco group stayed for more than twenty-five days, the longest any outside group had ever occupied a federal office building. In the end, Califano signed the regulation in advance of his deadline, and Eunice had her victory.

The section 504 regulation is without doubt the single most important document published in America on behalf of disabled people. It has become highly controversial because it calls for substantial expenses to remove barriers facing disabled people and to prevent discrimination of any kind in programs and activities funded fully or in part by the federal government. The HEW regulation served as the basis for similar regulations soon published by the Departments of Transportation, Labor, Treasury, and State, among other agencies, and extending protection for disabled people into virtually every segment of American life. For the first time, America's disabled population had explicit legal rights, rights they could be assured of in courts of law as well as by filing complaints with the federal government. It was a victory that stands with Title VI of the Civil Rights Act of 1964 as a major advance in the nation's treatment of its minorities. And it was a victory that was won, in large part, because Eunice Fiorito would not give up.

I first saw her incredible determination when she convinced me, against my better judgment, to apply for the job of ACCD director. It was a warm spring afternoon in May, 1976. We were sitting in her lower Manhattan office, where she directed the New York City Mayor's Office for the Handicapped. Eunice had called me there a half-dozen times already and we had spent perhaps twelve hours talking about ACCD and her dreams for the fledgling organization. Now she seemed to shift her attention from the organization to me. Opening her big, bright blue eyes in an expression of earnest candor, leaning forward with her elbows on the desk for emphasis, and speaking with exaggerated care because she thought it would help me lip-read her, she told me: "Frank, I want you to consider very carefully what I am about to say. I want you to come to Washington to direct the coalition."

I knew Eunice well enough by that time to have no illusions about my ability to persuade her that she should look elsewhere. Certainly, I had all the best reasons to decline her invitation. My wife Phyllis and I were happily settled in Greenwich Village and were expecting our first child that summer. I had just completed my doctoral studies in psychology at New York University and was looking forward to a career as a researcher in learning and memory. For both personal and professional reasons, then, I was hardly prepared for what Eunice frankly described as a twenty-hour-a-day job of tilting at windmills: establishing a headquarters office for a national organization virtually from scratch, attracting the funds that would be needed to operate that office and to hire staff, and battling the nation's top political officials for hotly controversial civil rights gains.

Eunice beat down every objection. Finally, she played her ace: the argument she knew I would not be able to deny. "Frank, if you leave your research into learning and memory for four or five years, won't people still learn and remember in the same ways when you come back to your research? That won't change, will it? But if you take this job, in four or five years, if you are even half the person I think you are, the lives of millions of Americans will be greatly improved. You will have changed their lives forever." It was flattery of the purest sort, but as someone who had also known discrimination on the basis of disability, I had to accept the challenge.

Such were the woman's persuasive powers that I wanted her to lead me on, to make me believe she was right about what this organization could do, and to challenge and drive me on to respond to her vision of me as ACCD's director. She made it clear that I need not adopt her tactics as a manipulator, but she left no doubt that she expected me to deal on the same level she did, and with the same results. And throughout my four years at ACCD, even after she had left as its president, she provided me with the support and guidance I needed to perform in the job.

ACCD was, and is, of great personal importance to Eunice. For her, it is the disability movement's counterpart to the National Association for the Advancement of Colored People (NAACP) and to the National Organization for Women (NOW). Acutely conscious of discrimination against her for much of her life, she believed that disabled people, like blacks and women, needed an organization that would fight for their rights. ACCD was in many ways her "baby": she conceived it as a cross-disability umbrella organization uniting the disparate and (at the time) squabbling groups of disabled people, nourished it when everyone she talked to told her it was an impossible dream, and guided it to maturity as a powerful advocate for the nation's 36 million disabled people.

When she first started talking up a coalition, cooperation among different groups of disabled people was rarely successful. People with physical impairments saw themselves as fundamentally different from those who had mental disabilities; similarly, deaf and blind people often viewed each other as competition. Eunice, almost alone, understood that if people with all kinds of disabilities worked together, their numbers would bring them real political power. Thirty-six million: they constituted the country's largest minority, and it was high time, she believed, that they started acting that way, insisting upon their rights and upon the political power she saw as their due. Almost no one believed that it could be done. They told Eunice it would never happen.

Crisscrossing the nation, from coast to coast and border to border, she spent most of 1973 and 1974 overcoming doubts about her vision. Along the way, she convinced other disabled leaders to sacrifice time, energy, and money to help her create the organization. These volunteers worked for almost three years to establish the foundation upon which ACCD would emerge. And when it did, they turned naturally to Eunice to be its first president. Six years later, she would form a second group, the League of Disabled Voters, to coalesce the voting strength of this minority and to cement the civil rights gains ACCD had made. But by this time, she understood that her real interests lay in creating something anew more than in administering an organization, so she declined to serve as LDV's president.

"I get *frustrated* with the slowness of change, and the slowness of people to change. We've come a long, long way, but we still have a very lengthy journey ahead of us. I am amazed and angered at how few people see me as a person. I am a human being who happens to be blind, not a blind being who happens to be human. But it is astounding how few people understand that. I don't think I will ever rest until they do— not just for me, but for all of us."

EUNICE K. FRELLY was born October 1, 1930, the second daughter of Joseph Frelly, a manager at International Harvester, and the former Anna Root. She remembers vividly, while she was growing up on Chicago's West Side, her father's exhortations to "try." Her parents were first-generation immigrants, her father from Poland and her mother from Germany. Neither had much education; her father had completed eighth grade and her mother third grade. They were upwardly mobile, hard-working people with, she says, "a great deal of pride and determination to 'get ahead.' "

Her father took great pride in the fact that he was never without a job, despite hard times during the depression. "He was a pusher from the word go. He started as a messenger for International Harvester and finished as one of their vicepresidents. His drive to 'have ladies for daughters' played a big role in making me what I am." Her bearing as a self-confident, even arrogant, person comes, she believes, from her father's repeated expressions of belief in her. If she got 95 on a test, he wanted to know why she didn't get 100. "I've never lost that determination," she says.

At birth, Eunice was given an overdose of silver nitrate in her eyes. She was diagnosed as blind at eight months. When she was one year old, one cataract was removed; another was removed at three. It was then that she experienced near-normal vision for the first time. It gave her tremendous confidence. "I became a great explorer at three. I rode my kiddie car like a bat out of hell. Life was so easy for me then. I had spoken at seven months and walked at eight months, so I was always regarded as somewhat precocious."

Even before she was three, her parents had made the decision to raise Eunice as though she were a sighted child. So strong were their views on the need for her to function "normally" that she has always had difficulty regarding herself as a blind person. "It was not until I was thirty-five and running the Mayor's Office for the Handicapped that I identified myself as a blind person for the first time."

She lost her sight permanently at the age of sixteen after a severe blow to her right eye. The diagnosis was glaucoma. "Apparently, the silver nitrate predisposed my eyes to 'something' and this was it. I was in terrible pain. A short time later, while Christmas shopping, I had a pain in my left eye. I closed it and discovered that I could not see at all with the right eye. That night, I woke up in pain, and found that the vision in my left eye was gone, too." It was, she remembers, December 8, 1946. She has not seen since.

Eunice completed her studies at Good Counsel High School, about one hundred blocks from her home, easily navigating the entire distance each day. "I've always been able to travel exceptionally well. Once I know a place, I know a place." It is a phenomenal skill. I have seen Eunice enter a hotel she has not been to in five years and immediately know her way around. We have visited friends who live in Byzantine apartment complexes with innumerable hallways, and Eunice invariably finds her way around better than I do. Said one cabdriver who occasionally takes her around town: "This lady is astounding. If I make one wrong turn, she knows it."

Her major concern in her high school days was, she remembers, belonging as a member of a group. "Being like the other kids was important. I wanted to be accepted as part of a group." She continued singing, which she loved. From the age of nine, she had been singing every other Sunday to prisoners at Cook

County jail, including those scheduled to be electrocuted the following day. At twelve, she was singing professionally. Being blind did not stop her from continuing. In fact, she says, she gave up only two things, but both were painful: driving and playing baseball.

"I was something of a tomboy. Even as a teen-ager, I was rather big. I would protect small kids, fat kids, and others who were picked on. It was part of my sense of responsibility. Growing up Catholic in a Catholic neighborhood, I was taught that we were responsible for each other. I believed very strongly in that. As a result, I never lacked for friends."

She was, she says, something of a "bigmouth." She gave the nuns and priests a hard time and would speak up forcefully if she believed she or someone she liked was being wrongly treated. "My parents never discouraged that; they never punished me for speaking up."

The blindness itself caused her relatively little concern. She remembers being more worried about how her family was reacting to the blindness than she was about herself. And she continues to be thankful to one nun in particular who insisted that she act as she had and be treated exactly as she had been before she lost her sight. "I called her Sister Pee Wee. She was hard as nails. She took my closest friend away from me lest I become too dependent upon her. Sister Pee Wee was determined that I was going to be independent. And, of course, as she always did, she got her way."

Eunice heard a radio advertisement about vocational rehabilitation, which lifted her hopes that she would be able to work despite blindness. These hopes were quickly dashed, however, as the agency took eighteen long months to process her application and certify her as eligible. "That was more painful and difficult for me than losing my sight, because it made me face the reality that there might not be a future for me."

Eunice then applied for and secured a job at the Chicago Lighthouse for the Blind. It was there that she earned five cents an hour assembling wires for telephones. Her bouncy, confident manner contrasted sharply with the defeatist mood of her co-workers. "They looked beaten. As individuals, they were too frightened to challenge what they knew was an unfair system." So Eunice organized them during lunch breaks, asking them to sing union songs with her. The Lighthouse management saw her as a troublemaker and encouraged her to attend college "in order to get rid of me." A blind social worker, Ethel Heeren, taught Eunice independent living skills to prepare her for college. "She tried to smooth over my rough edges without dampening my spirits."

Eunice proved a quick study. She mastered the difficult art of reading and writing Braille in just two weeks—an astounding feat I still have difficulty believing. Her independence, Braille skills, and that sonarlike travel ability enabled her to complete her bachelor's degree program at Loyola of Chicago in just three years, earning a B.A. in education *cum laude* in 1954.

She spent the next four years as a counseling and rehabilitation teacher for the Illinois State Department of Public Welfare. Employed by the department's Special Services for Visually Handicapped Persons Division, Eunice provided home instruction in mobility skills for newly blinded individuals, offered individual and family counseling, and developed community resources for aging and multiply handicapped blind people in the Chicago area.

A typical day saw her cover twenty miles, about three of them on foot, as she called on four to five clients, giving each an hour's lesson or travel test. After nine to ten hours on the job, Eunice would go to Loyola's School of Social Work for evening courses. It is a rigorous regimen she has maintained ever since. "I'm always up at six or six-thirty in the morning, on the go all day, and don't sleep until about two the next morning." As someone who has worked closely with Eunice for a period of several years, I can testify to the accuracy of that statement.

In 1958, Eunice decided to move to New York in order to complete her master's degree in social work at the prestigious Columbia University School of Social Work. For almost two years, she concentrated upon course work and her internship experiences at Roosevelt Hospital and the Jewish Guild for the Blind. She was doing work few others had ever done: providing psychiatric social work services to blind children with emotional disturbances. The field was so new, in fact, that the fifty-year-old guild began its program during Eunice's term there. After receiving her M.S.W. from Columbia, Eunice became a social worker at the guild, responsible for a caseload of about forty-five families in each of which at least one member was blind. In addition to providing individual and group counseling, she did school and vocational planning and interagency program coordination and gave numerous public speeches about the agency and its services. Hers was the first psychiatric social work program for blind people in the nation.

Her work with clients usually began with a battery of tests to assist in diagnosing the problem. Eunice would then visit the family at home in order to understand the family dynamics more completely. "I had to use myself as a tool to find out how people feel about themselves and about each other before I could begin to help them." It was during her three-year stint at the guild that she met and married James Fiorito, a sighted printer. Although the marriage did not last more than a few years, she and her ex-husband remain close friends. The problem, Eunice says, was her devotion to her career; she never really gave the marriage sufficient chance to work.

Anxious not to be typecast as a "blind social worker," Eunice followed another former guild employee to New York University's Bellevue Hospital Center, beginning as a senior psychiatric social worker responsible for intake evaluation and program planning for children and their families. She concentrated upon children with autism, developing case histories, conducting psychosocial assessments, and providing therapy to the families.

She remembers her first day at Bellevue: January 6, 1964. Eunice walked into the clinic for the first time and was immediately shown her first client. "I didn't even know where my office was. So with my coat on, I walked out, introduced myself, and did the interview right there on the bench. I don't recall much else about it except that I was outraged that the clinic was so poorly organized. It was a terribly dingy place. The patients were overdrugged to keep them quiet, but no one seemed to know how to accept them as human beings with problems. I think the whole staff had some difficulty with me and my blindness, but the medical students in particular just could not get it through their heads that a social worker who was blind could do the kinds of things I was doing.

"I really began to complain—about the rats on the wards with the children, about the constant dirt and filth, and the way no one did anything about it. So one day I got a bunch of students together and we got the kids to help us and we really cleaned that place up. We painted it in bright, cheerful colors. That was the beginning."

The hospital administrators were sufficiently impressed by her professionalism to promote her to psychiatric social work supervisor, responsible for a staff of eleven, program planning and development, and supervision of graduate social work students. The clinic was one of the largest of its kind in the world. "I was asked to reorganize the clinic and to get it relicensed. It had lost its state license and nobody knew it!"

Eunice lost no time in transferring inept personnel out of the clinic and bringing in new people who cared about quality services. She set up a community mental health unit, a group therapy program, and family therapy sessions. She inaugurated in-service training to ensure that the staff kept up-to-date on developments in social work.

No sooner had she secured a new license for the program than she was asked to become acting director of social work and rehabilitation. She accepted the assignment on the condition that she get the job on a permanent basis within three months or she would return to the clinic. On the day before her deadline, no decision had been made. So the social work staff organized the entire Bellevue Hospital Center professional staff to demonstrate at the hospital, insisting that she be named permanent director. It was a measure of their recognition that she had returned the program to respectability and that continued progress required her being in that job. "I was overwhelmed," she recalls.

She did not waste time getting on with her work. First, she worked toward getting the entire hospital and all its wards painted in cheerful colors. Then she recommended abolition of the policy of requiring patients to wear hospital garb and had them wear their own clothes instead. She instituted real work activity for the patients, believing that constructive work would help in their therapy. She helped develop a program to allow patients to leave the hospital to engage in community activities. And she brought vocational rehabilitation counselors into the hospital to help the patients plan their careers. She developed group work, community organizing, and student training programs at the hospital. To her, perhaps the most important step was the improvement of working relationships among the different professionals on the wards.

During her six years at Bellevue, Eunice always tried "to keep my hand in personal client services." One child she remembers fondly was diagnosed as autistic. "Shelly was about seven. I used to come in daily just to talk to Shelly for about fifteen minutes. There was never a response from her; no one could get any response. After a solid year and a half of talking to Shelly and not getting any reaction, I brought with me a kids' book and told Shelly how much I wished I could read that book, but couldn't because I couldn't see. I was dumfounded and amazed when she took the book and started reading it to me. And that's how we broke through to her. I can't tell you what that meant to me. It's without question one of the most outstanding successes Eunice Fiorito ever had."

It was at about this time that Eunice first became active politically. Enactment of a state law creating mental retardation programs to be operated by private associations offended her because she believed strongly that public services should be provided by public agencies as well as by private, voluntary agencies. Eunice organized an intense lobby that changed the law, resulting in establishment of a city-sponsored program in Manhattan. "I had by that time come to the conclusion that there was only so much I could do within the confines of a hospital. Many of the problems disabled people have are a result of political actions. So the solutions to these problems must be found in the political arena."

In 1970, she left Bellevue to coordinate the newly formed Mayor's Advisory Committee on the Handicapped. Three years later, the committee was upgraded to become the Mayor's Office for the Handicapped, and Eunice was named director. It was in this position that she began to function as an advocate for disabled people within government. When President Richard Nixon vetoed a $2.6 billion rehabilitation bill to aid handicapped people, Eunice organized four busloads of New Yorkers in a "persuasion pilgrimage" to Washington in an attempt to convince Congress to override the veto. That effort served both the city, which stood to gain funds if the bill passed, and disabled people. But the congruence of interests would not always be there.

When Eunice lobbied in Washington three years later for a strong section 504 regulation, for example, or when she fought for full access to transportation for disabled and elderly people, New York City's interests did not always match those of the disabled. Section 504 and transportation access both cost money, which by that time was in extremely short supply in New York. Eunice's philosophy was to follow her instincts— and to explain later. And I have no doubt that she was able to explain each act to the full and complete satisfaction of the mayor and his chief aides. Eunice has that ability.

"The big problem in New York was that disabled people were totally disorganized. To a distressing degree, they still are. What I tried to do at the mayor's office was to make sure the groups knew what was going on and that the city knew their views on active issues. We brought together consumers, professionals, and parents to work with the city agencies in planning services, budgets, and legislative priorities. We also did a lot of information-and-referral work for individual disabled people. There are supposed to be a million such people in and around the city. It's amazing how little we know about their needs and how little they know about our services."

Just as she had become frustrated at Bellevue, believing that she could do much more in city politics, so too the mayor's office soon seemed more confining than liberating. The real action, she decided, was in Washington. So in the summer of 1976, she flew to Atlanta to meet with a young lawyer named Stuart Eizenstat, who was domestic policy adviser to Democratic presidential candidate Jimmy Carter. Eunice came away from the meeting with the heady title of co-chair of Carter's Disability Policy Committee.

Eighteen months later, she was named special assistant to the commissioner of rehabilitation services in HEW, in Washington, D.C. Just before accepting the appointment, Eunice tendered her resignation as ACCD president in order to avoid even the appearance of conflict of interest.

Washington has not been as much fun for Eunice as she had hoped it might be. The massive bureaucracy often moves with stupefying slowness, leading Eunice, ever the active go-getter, to tears of frustration. Her reputation as an advocate had preceded her to Washington, which made relations with some longstanding federal bureaucrats difficult. She misses the flexibility she enjoyed in New York—and the freedom to fight the good fights. But none of that stops her from being an agitator, a civil rights leader, and, yes, a hellion.

EUNICE BELIEVES that her most important contribution to the nation's disabled population has been to help them become more politically sophisticated, organized, and powerful. "Today's disabled consumers are no longer content to sit back and let others run their lives, plan their futures, or otherwise make decisions on their behalf. Today's consumers are no longer content to sell pencils on street corners, weave baskets in sheltered workshops, or take jobs beneath their capacities. Millions of disabled Americans are demanding, and getting, greater control over the decisions and conditions affecting their lives.

"As disabled persons become politically aware, they realize that their apparent second-class status stems not so much from their own inabilities as from society's inability or unwillingness to accommodate their special needs. The prejudice they face is far more subtle than the outright bigotry encountered by ethnic minorities in their own liberation struggles. The answers, too, are more elusive: barrier removal, certainly, but also altering society's perceptions of disabled people from persons who *can't* to persons who *can.*"

These are, she believes, political problems demanding political solutions. And she has some interesting ideas about where those solutions will be found.

Eunice is a big believer in governmental advocacy. In this, she differs radically from many advocates who persist in seeing government as the enemy. She has especially high hopes for her profession of social work. "Social workers are caught between an unyielding social welfare bureaucracy and a service population whose needs and aspirations have outgrown the services being provided. Social work must change to meet these altered demands. Today's social worker must no longer be a dispenser of charity, but rather an ally, an advocate, a catalyst, and often a prime mover in a disabled client's struggle for independence. Through traditional community organizing skills, a politically knowledgeable worker can form a bond among otherwise disunited members of a disabled population, thus forging a politically active unit eager to confront the problems that draw them together while overlooking the differences that set them apart." Eunice's career clearly exemplifies these convictions.

She sees government as being designed to ensure the rights of and provide services to people through implementation and enforcement of laws. This role includes advocacy, with input and support from the population being served. When I asked her to define the seemingly contradictory term "governmental advocacy," Eunice had a reply ready: "A method, practiced within a governmental setting, which uses a variety of skills and techniques within a planned programmatic framework. This should be designed to accomplish specific goals and objectives related to the population for which it is advocating. It can have two phases. One is internal advocacy, or work within the agency to enable it to act more responsively toward meeting the needs of the population. The second is external advocacy, or advocacy that stimulates other agency programs to become more responsive." Eunice had given a lot of thought to that definition, having worked as an advocate in government for more than ten years.

As special assistant to the commissioner of rehabilitation services in the federal Education Department, Eunice has implemented this definition by stressing consumer involvement in governmental decision making. She has sought to identify disabled leaders nationwide, bring them up-to-date on policy questions being considered by the department, solicit their considered advice, and help them gain a hearing from the top officials in the department. She has also stressed in-service training for departmental workers, sensitizing them to disability and to the needs of disabled people, acquainting them with advocacy techniques and skills, and helping them to advocate improved services. She has helped her agency to work more closely with the federal bodies responsible for implementing and enforcing civil rights, so that rehabilitation and civil rights personnel collaborate in offering a full range of services to disabled people. In particular, she believes that rehabilitation professionals, because of their long involvement in helping disabled individuals solve employment-related problems, are a natural resource for civil rights officials in solving complex implementation and enforcement questions. For instance, what is reasonable accommodation? How can a deaf person's communication needs best be met? And what kinds of accommodations will best serve an individual with cerebral palsy?

Another of Eunice's deep convictions is that disabled people need to reach out to other minorities, joining ranks with them in common struggles for improved civil rights. Under her leadership, ACCD forged a close working relationship with the Leadership Conference on Civil Rights, an association of 167 organizations, churches, and unions committed to equality of opportunity. Its chairman, Clarence Mitchell, the long-time Washington bureau head of the NAACP, proved a tremendous ally. Eunice also worked hard on various women's groups, seeking to enlist their aid for disabled women. She was a delegate to the International Women's Year Conference in Houston in 1977, co-authoring the section on rights of disabled women included in the U.S. Women's Plan for Action. Three years later, she served as a delegate representing the United States at the Copenhagen World Conference of the United Nations Decade for Women.

Whatever she is doing and wherever she is going, Eunice enthusiastically practices what she preaches. Asked by an airline ticket agent, "When will you people stop trying to fly by yourselves?" she promptly took her ticket to a competing airline and booked herself on one of their flights. When the Pope visited America in 1979, Eunice loudly complained that disabled people were not being permitted equal access to papal masses. "I felt very strongly that if the Church says we are equal, and the Pope says we are supposed to show love to all people, the Church ought to practice what it preaches. I told that to about six Monsignors." Addressing an international meeting of scientists, engineers, and others who design tools and devices for disabled people, Eunice blasted them for failing to consult consumers about what they want and need: "Hundreds of thousands of devices are made throughout the world every year that disabled people can't use. Consult us. After all, we're in the best position to say what we need in the way of better wheelchairs, reading machines, living quarters, or public transportation."

And what does Eunice, the consummate independent and self-sufficient disabled woman, want?

"Oh, I'd really like some device to help me apply nail polish without getting it all over my hands."

2

SUSAN DANIELS

"My question is not 'Why me?' but
'What next?' "

THIRTY-TWO-YEAR-OLD SUSAN DANIELS stands front and center in one of the most explosive areas of human interaction: that of sex counseling for severely disabled individuals. Sexuality and disability are emotionally loaded terms, generating, even during the supposedly enlightened eighties, intense and often conflicting feelings. Combining the two, as when a cerebral-palsied woman confronts her sexuality for the first time, often produces anxiety and confusion among parents, professionals, laymen, and disabled persons themselves.

Susan knows this: she has met and dealt with her own sexual being during adolescence and early adulthood. She has faced the aching need for simple respect as a person, one of the most basic aspects of human sexuality. She has confronted the need to force people to recognize her as a woman, and not just as a sexually neuter person with a disability. She has wrestled with her image of herself, discarding the "child" image thrust upon her, and developing instead a self-image joining her sense of herself as a sexual being with her vision of herself as a professional researcher and teacher. And she has come to terms with her body, ravaged as it is by polio, reveling in its responsiveness and erogeneity while respecting its limits and needs.

You can sense the depth of Susan's feeling of achievement at having made it through all of this to a renewed confidence in herself as a woman. You can see it in her posture and bearing, a standing tall, neither hiding her body out of shame nor flaunting it out of defiance. But most of all, you can sense it in her eyes. Susan's big green eyes are undoubtedly her most arresting feature—bright, blazingly honest, and inquisitive. They captivate, they exude candor and invite honesty, and they challenge you to look into yourself as you know she has looked into herself.

She needs those eyes in her chosen profession. As head of the Department of Rehabilitation Counseling at Louisiana State

University's Medical Center, Susan Daniels teaches students and practitioners in human services fields how to counsel disabled individuals about their sexuality. And she does her own counseling, with a private caseload, helping severely disabled people identify their sexual needs and act to satisfy these long-denied yearnings. Whether talking to professionals or to disabled people, Susan must establish a climate of complete acceptance, an atmosphere of uncritical interest and support. And she must move beyond that to challenge her students and clients to confront head-on their own highly ambiguous feelings about sexuality and disability. Those big, probing green eyes at once accept and challenge: I understand, they seem to be saying, but look further into yourself and tell me if you really feel that way and if you are comfortable with that feeling.

Susan is able to do that even in the company of very severely disabled persons who are light-years away psychologically from successful adjustment to their sexuality. She can support others and expect from them as she does because she's been there herself. She has traveled the distance.

Susan's disabilities kept her away from her family for nine of her first fifteen months of life. That kind of separation, at so tender an age, can produce devastating scars and permanent wounds to a child's sense of self. Susan survived that. She underwent several hours of physical therapy every day for seventeen years, fighting a body that just would not respond as it should. During these formative years, she was forced to concentrate upon what was wrong with her body—for some eighteen thousand hours. Even after each day's therapy, she was continually reminded of her body, constantly shown how it differed from the perfectly formed bodies of girls and women around her. Again, so intensive and extensive a searing experience could only make her highly sensitive to what is wrong with her. Yet again, Susan overcame that. For the first twenty-three years of her life, she traveled with the aid of a wheelchair, a golf cart, or some other device, continually looking up at others, always aware of her differentness. And once again, she rose above that.

So she feels confident, and conveys that confidence, however wrenching or hopeless a client or a case may appear. She knows what it is like. She has been there. And she has survived worse.

When a client talks about viewing his body "as a sack of potatoes," Susan knows what he means. When another says she is ashamed to talk about her desire for sexual stimulation "because I'm not supposed to have these feelings," Susan knows what she is saying. When a woman complains that "I've never been treated like a girl or like a woman," Susan can identify with the feelings being expressed. The acceptance is there. The green eyes tell you that. But then Susan can help her client past these negative emotions and experiences and begin to turn them around. The challenge to self-examination is there. It's in her eyes.

"If you can get through adolescence without going crazy, then the rest of it is easy sailing. It's in the teen years when you sit at home and say, 'I'm as smart and as pretty and as charming as my girl friends, but I'm the one at home waiting for the phone to ring.' That's when you wonder why you're different," she says. "Adolescence," she adds, pausing to consider the word, "now, that's a killer."

The irony, and the bitterness, for Susan is that it is in precisely these years that no one offers the honesty and the help that is needed. Teachers, parents, even counselors are uncomfortable with sexuality in disabled students, so the subject is avoided, hidden, rejected. And the adolescent is left alone to grapple with massively conflicting emotions. On the one hand are the powerful biological and social desires and drives. On the other are the messages, coming from all sides, that sexual appeal equals physical attractiveness. The teen-ager cannot turn on the television, pick up a magazine, or go to a shopping center without being bombarded with that message. And no one is there to say that there is more to sexuality than physical beauty.

No one is there to help you find something attractive in yourself, something to feel good about, and something to develop
and use to attract others. And so the teen concludes, entirely
logically, that he or she is asexual, unsexual, or nonsexual.

Susan believes that the real tragedy is that these feelings
of rejection generalize very quickly. Attitudes toward sexuality
are central to attitudes toward almost everything else as well.
And so negative experiences during adolescence can destroy
the very self-confidence that the teen most needs to find academic, vocational, and personal success in other areas of life.
It is not surprising, then, to find Susan approaching the sexual
problems of people with disabilities as one aspect of the more
general problem of attitudes toward disability itself. She sees
these attitudes as perhaps the greatest barrier facing people
who are disabled. Much of her work, then, has been in the
area of helping people to become aware of their own attitudes
and to change these. She does this work at LSU in her classes,
in speeches around the country, and in workshops she conducts
at association conventions and conferences.

Watching her in these sessions, I was struck by her skill at
drawing people out to discuss things they would not otherwise
talk about. Standing—or, more frequently, sitting—in a room
with a few dozen people, she projects relaxation, interest in
her students, and a quiet determination to get to the heart
of the matter, to help people past their initial apprehensions.

Susan knows that attitudes are intensely personal emotions
and beliefs, and that revealing them honestly can be difficult
for many people. This is particularly true when the discussion
is about sexuality. Combining disability and sexuality, and leading the students to talk about themselves in that context, takes
real skill and genuine talent. She has to create just the right
setting in that room, just the exact delicate balance between
prurience on the one hand and self-conscious silence on the
other.

Her green eyes sparkling beneath her close-cropped,

bleached-blond hair, she will say "I" repeatedly, not shrinking from the personal and the immediate. Her sentences are short and declarative. I have never heard Susan take refuge behind academic jargon or the subjunctive mood of protective obscurity. Slowly, almost imperceptibly, she will begin using the word "I" to refer not to herself but to her students. "Why do I feel that way? Ask yourself: how would I react in that situation?" she will ask, probing softly, pausing patiently but firmly to encourage responses from the participants. And she will prompt her students to move from such impersonal pronouns as "one" and "you" to "I." When the discussion meanders away from the subject, as it often does when a student is struggling with his or her feelings, she may call upon another student and pose the question at hand in a direct manner, leaving no doubt that she wants to keep the discussion on target—and then, later, come back to the student who was having difficulty, finding ways to help that student work through his or her feelings. It comes as no surprise after seeing Susan at work to learn that one of her favorite words is "gentle." She will use it to describe her grandmother, her mother, and her brothers and sisters, as well as others close to her. And it is clear that "gentle" is one of the words that helps describe Susan herself.

The same traits of comforting decisiveness and firm acceptance serve her well in counseling sessions. A woman who suffered a spinal cord injury while swimming will complain of lacking all sensation below her waist. She will want to have sexual satisfaction and be bewildered about how she is supposed to do that when she feels virtually nothing in her vaginal area. Susan knows how to help this woman identify erogenous zones in other parts of her body, how to ask the woman to explain what does give her pleasure. The answer for this woman might not be the traditional missionary position, but there is an answer and she can find satisfaction in a sexual relationship. Susan will be definite about that while being accepting about what the woman describes as her limits. Together, they will find answers.

As traumatic as that first sexual act without sensation might be, following the onset of disability, and as frightening as it may be to confront the reality that this is what it will be like from here on out, Susan knows her clients need a range of supportive services and various kinds of assistance. She realizes that the mechanics of sexual unions, the cookbook approaches so popular today, are but a small part of the solutions her clients need and seek. Rather, help in making overall psychological adjustment to disability, in reconstructing a positive sense of self, and in managing the social aspects of a relationship can be just as important as the mere mechanics, or more so. And the reverse is equally true: when sexual adjustment is achieved, overall psychological adjustment improves as well. It is by viewing the client as a complete human being, not as a case with a malfunctioning part or with a discrete problem, that Susan believes she can be most helpful.

Perhaps the first step, possibly the most important, is recognizing and respecting the humanity and the sexuality of the person. For someone who has just become disabled, that may be the hardest step to take. But even people who have been disabled since infancy may need considerable help in viewing themselves accurately, positively, and acceptingly, if only because the people around them during their childhood and adolescence did not give them that sense of self. It is rarely possible for someone to have healthy sexual relationships until he or she understands and accepts himself or herself.

Just as Plato said, "Know thyself," expressing a powerful truth—that people cannot view other people or ideas with objectivity until they are able to separate themselves from what they are studying—so, in a more modest way, Susan might say, "Love thyself," as a way of suggesting that you cannot love someone else until you like and, yes, love yourself. This is not narcissism; rather, it is an essential element of what most major psychoanalysts, certainly Erich Fromm but also Anna Freud, recognize as comprising the ability to be a loving person.

For someone who is disabled, and who has seen the way others around him respond to that disability, self-acceptance can be excruciatingly difficult. It is only too easy to internalize the negative reactions of others. Susan draws upon her personal experience in helping clients through this critical stage. "My own sexual development was pushed along by several loving men in my late teens and early twenties," she recalls. "I was very lucky that they took me as I was. By accepting me, they helped me accept myself."

Susan leads three-day seminars at LSU three times each year; they begin with a discussion of some of the myths about sexuality and disability. Among these myths are perceptions that can harm a disabled person's self-concept and ability to live independently as well as beliefs that lead others around the disabled individual to restrict or hinder his or her personal development. One such myth is that disabled persons are asexual. "In essence, the disabled person is regarded as a neuter who does not have the same needs, desires, and capabilities as others," Susan explains. The opposite myth, particularly prevalent among the general public when mental retardation is discussed, is that disabled people are oversexed and have uncontrollable urges. This myth is a holdover from the eugenics scare of the early 1900s in this country, which produced many state laws on involuntary sterilization of retarded and other disabled people. The same movement also created a third myth: that disability breeds disability. The movement produced a fear among the general population that "defectives" might breed more "defectives" in such numbers that eventually they would outnumber "normals." A rash of laws prohibiting marriage and procreation among disabled people resulted.

Other myths hold that the disabled individuals are childlike (the "eternal child myth," Susan calls it) people who need to be protected from knowledge about and experience with sexuality. Thus, one meets parents with disabled children now in their twenties, yet the parents persist in denying sexuality in their children. An incident involving such sexuality might produce outrage and violent punishment by the parent. Similarly, there is a myth that disabled people are better off and more comfortable with others who are disabled. This is the "their own kind" myth. Finally, we have the myth holding that if a disabled person has sexual problems, these are almost always the result of the disability rather than of other factors.

Susan explored these myths in a volume she wrote with several other authors at George Washington University, a landmark manuscript in this field called *Who Cares? A Handbook on Sex Education and Counseling Services for Disabled People.* A report of the Sex & Disability Project sponsored by the Rehabilitation Services Administration and George Washington, this manual reflects the belief of Susan Daniels and her colleagues that sexuality is best understood as the integration of all aspects of an individual's personality which express maleness or femaleness. This definition immediately rules out the conception that sexuality occurs only in the bedroom (or in the back seat of a car) in favor of a broader view which sees sexuality expressed in work, socialization, decoration of a home, telephone conversations, child rearing, expressions of affection, and even eating a meal.

From that kind of a framework, Susan's views about the centrality of sexuality in work with disabled people become understandable. "The issue of sexuality is a very clear barometer of our progress toward normalization," she says. "Where progress has been made, it is because disabled people are seen in a humane and equal light. Where progress has been resisted, it is directly linked to a controlling, dehumanizing environment. Sexuality is also one of the ways a person can express self-esteem and self-advocacy. As a medium of rehabilitation, it offers a channel for developing joyous self-respect, something disabled people are often robbed of; some gain self-respect but no joy. Fun is vastly, and I mean vastly, underrated in rehabilitation. Those brave souls who are always overcoming their disabilities seldom have the space, or the chance, to *be* overcome—to play, to have fun, to have orgasms, to be sensuous, to let go."

SUSAN REMEMBERS her childhood, if not her adolescence, as a time of joy despite her disabilities. Susan Daniels was born October 24, 1948, in Navy Hospital, New Orleans, to Harry and Marie Daniels. Her father was a police officer, and would later become chief of detectives, while her mother was "the epitome of the 1940s–1950s mother, her life centered around the family." Susan was the last-born of the family's four children.

Home for the Danielses was a parkside house on Sherwood Forest Drive in New Orleans. Her parents were active participants in the neighborhood parish, sending all four children to parochial schools. Susan remembers her father as "Irish, I guess that's the best way to describe him. He was always being told that he acted like Spencer Tracy. He was boisterous and colorful, but very dedicated to his work." Her mother Susan describes as "an energetic, fun-loving woman, thoroughly devoted to her children. My mother has one criterion for behavior: is it good for my child? In addition to this, she has an assertive, definitive view of herself. My mother can in no way be intimidated. I daresay, if intimidating is going on, she's doing it."

Susan remembers her relationship with her older sister Mary as being one of competition and mutual irritation. "I was always wanting to play with her make-up and to sit with her when her friends came to talk. I am sure she thought me an awful bother." It is a relationship that has become much closer now that both are adults. "When Mary left home to marry, I rejoiced! My own room at last, and no big sister to call me 'silly.' " Looking back, Susan believes her sister, like her older brother Harry, might have been envious of the attention she received because of her physical problems. "But today, Mary and I are very close. It took several years, long hours of sharing and exchanging feelings, as well as several good cries, but we did it, and we have a closeness now, a real sisterhood, with deep mutual affection."

Susan's brother Ernie was the oldest child as well as the biggest. She remembers him as the most social of the four Daniels children, gregarious, well-read, and compassionate. He was large even as a youth, and today stands six feet three and weighs 280 pounds. By the time Susan reached the torturous teen years, he had already left home. The second child was Harry, a quiet and gentle boy of whom Susan says: "He was a hippie before hippies were a social phenomenon. He was shy, tender, and personally lovely."

Susan began life inauspiciously, her left hip malformed at birth. The problem was not noticed until she started to walk. But at six months, Susan contracted polio in a summer epidemic, and the event traumatized the family. Quarantined in the hospital for three months, she could not have visitors. "It was a difficult time for my parents," she says. "My mother almost left my father during one particularly bitter fight. Watching me from the elevator for brief moments—that was as close as they were permitted to get—my father suggested that if I could not breathe by myself, without the aid of machines, I should be allowed to die. That really set my mother off."

Susan eventually recovered well enough to spend some time at home. But barely two weeks out of the hospital, she departed for Warm Springs, Georgia, for physical therapy at that town's famous rehabilitation center. Susan was there for six months.

When she returned, she remembers, "My brothers thought of me as a new doll. They didn't consider me a baby, or their sister, because I had been gone so long." At the age of fifteen months, she did not even recognize her mother. The family hired a young German woman, Inge Rossolet, to do physical therapy with Susan.

"Inge was important to me," Susan says. "She spent so much time with me in therapy, back stretching and swimming, that she became almost a second mother for me." The physical therapy sessions lengthened gradually as Susan's strength developed, eventually reaching three hours each day. The attention of Inge and both parents added more tension to an already nervous household. Harry was just eighteen months older than Susan; the strain caused him to run away at one point. "He just hated me then," Susan says.

At three, Susan began trying to walk. It was then that her parents noticed the congenital hip dislocation, which prevented her from putting weight on her left foot. "I was already in a wheelchair because of the polio and was late learning to walk anyway, so there was nothing obvious that would have called attention to the hip earlier."

With continued physical therapy daily, Susan began making progress. The effort was strenuous, yet Susan remembers those years as joyful. She particularly reveled in her large extended family—thirty-one cousins, dozens of aunts and uncles, as well as her maternal grandmother, all of whom were regularly visiting with the Daniels family. "I've always felt close to all of these people. There is one question I've never pondered: where is home? Home is wherever 'we' are."

But it was not all smooth and easy. "I didn't notice it until much later, but when I was about seven or eight, my father really began drinking a lot. Whether it was my disability or the pressure of his work with the police I don't know for sure. Probably some of both. He continued to have a real alcohol problem until he died. In fact, when I was applying for college, one of the major reasons I looked for a school far away was to get away from alcohol."

Susan remembers one incident illustrating the attitude her parents, particularly her mother, took toward her disabilities.

Telling me about it, Susan explained that she had as a child an intense dislike of being stared at. "I developed a number of rather obnoxious maneuvers to express my disapproval of the starers, ranging from sticking out my tongue to asking them if they had been reared in a barn." One day, she and her mother were shopping in the local A&P when a woman approached, stared at Susan, and asked her mother: "What's the matter with your child?" Mrs. Daniels just looked down at Susan in her tiny wheelchair and inquired softly: "Is there anything the matter, Susan?" Receiving Susan's nervous "No," Mrs. Daniels looked the woman in the eye and said that, no, there was nothing the matter. Looking back, Susan admires her mother for being so unflappable: "I'm sure that woman thought mom was unfortunate having such a handicapped child but doubly unfortunate to be so insane."

The same attitudes served the Danielses well when it came time to consider a school for Susan. She calls them "very wise" in deciding to send her to the same school her older brothers and sister attended. "They could have said: 'Oh, we have this cripple, so we'll keep her inside and hidden.' Or they could have sent me to a special school. But they didn't. It is so important to me that my mother, and my father, too, never devalued me in private or in public. They were not the sort of people you'd want to take on in a battle, and they made it clear that if you messed with me, you'd have to take them on, too."

Susan has strong feelings about being segregated from the mainstream of society, and particularly about educational programs that separate disabled children from other children. "I think special schools are bad for children because there are later no special worlds for them to live in." It is a belief she clearly got from her parents. The decision was quickly made to enroll Susan in the parochial school her siblings attended, a decision made much easier by the ready concurrence of the kindergarten teacher. "She said: 'Sure, I'll take her,' just like that. It was a small school and the teacher made the decision, not the principal. She did, and I had no real problems there."

She remembers the rest of her childhood as happy and relatively uneventful. She had a boyfriend in second grade, brothers and sisters to watch out for her, and neighborhood friends who accepted her as a friend and a peer. "I was surrounded by people I knew and liked," she recalls. "It was just an average childhood."

Shortly after Susan entered first grade, her mother came to terms with the disability, acknowledging that it would not easily and quickly go away. "Mother talked about going to Lourdes someday, to cure me, but she stopped that when I was seven or eight. A few years ago, we were in Portugal and made a point of stopping in France to see Lourdes. She hated it! We talked about how foolish and silly the people coming there for cures were. My mother looked at the scene with disgust and remarked: 'They should build a rehabilitation center here instead.' "

Adolescence, on the other hand, was "dreadful. I had an awful time growing up. Adolescence for me was a mess." She still had a large circle of friends and the "vast extended family," but suddenly they were not enough. She attended St. Mary's Dominican High School, a college-prep school for girls run by nuns, and she enjoyed the academic life and the challenge of competing with nondisabled students. But life outside the classroom, with the constant talk of boys, the endless stream of parties and get-togethers, was closed to Susan. "I was lonely and wanted to date." Instead, she sat home alone, having a hard time taking the continuing rejection. "I got through it with the help of Inge, my mother, and other members of my family. They kept saying: 'This will get better.' And it did. Once I realized that I was not the only person in the world who had a monumental inconvenience—and who, please tell me, hasn't had a disabled life of some kind?—then I was better able to cope." She joined the debate team and the glee club, forcing herself to participate in as many social situations as she could, if only to take her mind off herself and her problems.

The teen years, she remembers, saw girls becoming very conscious of their appearance, changing their values to stress beauty and popularity. Differentness is scorned, conformity prized. Susan's disabilities assumed a role larger than ever before simply because they made her "different." And boys never called her for dates.

Susan was glad when she left for Marquette University, hoping that college students would be more mature, and looking forward, too, to proving that she could live independently. She almost didn't make it through her first semester. "I learned right away that I couldn't function on my own," she recalls. "I was almost thrown out after two months because I couldn't take care of myself." Fortunately, Jane Paelini, another student, volunteered to room with Susan. Susan will never forget Jane: "She helped me so much during that transition period, helping me to become more independent. I don't know what I would have done without her."

Living independently meant a number of things for Susan. She stopped wearing dresses with zippers in the back because she could not zip herself up. At home, there had always been someone to do that. "Needless to say, I haven't had a dress with a zipper since." She also cut her hair short so she would not have to roll it up. To get around the sprawling campus, Susan took to riding a golf cart. By that time, Susan cared less about how she looked than she did about the practicality of the cart. She needed it to live independently, so she used it. The cart was to stay with her throughout her undergraduate and graduate years.

Then came an event so important Susan still remembers the exact date: October 19, 1972. She had just begun her graduate studies at Mississippi State University. Her physical pains had become so intense that she was taking large doses of medication, particularly aspirin, but codeine as well. "It made me sleepy, of course, but it also made me forget things. I would just forget so much. And I had so little energy." She doubts she could have gone further in her education or even continued to live independently.

That October she entered Touro Hospital in New Orleans for hip replacement surgery.

"Suddenly, I had incredible amounts of energy. For weeks after the surgery, people would ask me if I was on uppers. And I would laugh and say: 'No, I'm off downers.' " The biggest change for her was simple mobility. She could walk now, not just one step, but virtually anywhere. The effect was remarkable and so sudden that her family and friends had difficulty adjusting. "I was different now and even my mother, driving me to a shopping center, couldn't understand what it meant. She would still hunt for a parking space right in front of the store, as she always had. I had to tell her to stop it, that I could walk now."

Returning to Mississippi State, she found her studies progressing much more easily and rapidly, her energy level still unbelievably high, and the constant pain a thing of the past. She was thinking and acting differently, too. One result of the change was her decision to end a relationship with a fellow student. "I was going nowhere fast in that relationship. It was time to move on." She also found her interests coalescing now around special education and rehabilitation. For her internship that summer, she taught a course on the psychology of mental retardation at the university.

It was an interest she had not always had. Susan still remembers her bitterness at being dissuaded from her original love, medicine. From her school days, she had been fascinated with things that grow, and this interest had matured gradually to a desire to work in the area of obstetrics and gynecology, with a specialty in high-risk mothers. At Marquette, she had taken a premedical curriculum. Finding the school as conservative in many ways as high school had been, she spent long hours with her roommates and other students during which they gave one another sexual counseling and contraceptive information. The whole area fascinated her, and she was determined to go to medical school in order to devote her career to this field.

Every medical school she approached rebuffed her, some even refusing to take an application. The rejection infuriated Susan. "I had the grades, a 3.89 average out of a possible 4.0, and high scores on the medical school admission test, so it was not a question of meeting admission criteria. And I had a burning desire to be a doctor, so it wasn't lack of motivation. I literally begged, and for me that's not easy to do. I begged to be given one year to prove myself, just a chance. But they turned me down flat." One school even sent her a letter saying they would not admit a student in a wheelchair.

Susan believes it was her disability that produced the rejections, but she also points out that it could have been her sex as well. "These were all southern universities, and the attitudes in those days were pretty strong against women becoming professionals." At the time, Title IX, which prohibits educational institutions from discriminating on the basis of sex, and section 504, which bars discrimination on the basis of disability, were not yet law. If they had been in effect, Susan believes, she would have sued to gain admission. "I've never forgiven them. Not that they ruined my life, I'm happy doing what I am doing. But this was my choice. I wanted to be a doctor. And I was as qualified and as motivated as the students they admitted."

She enrolled at Mississippi State for a master's degree in psychology as much to give herself time as for any other reason. The following year, she applied once again to medical schools, and once again was turned down. By this time, she had developed an interest in rehabilitation counseling, particularly sex counseling for disabled persons, as a field that came as close to high-risk obstetrics as anything. It is a decision she does not regret.

Susan began her doctoral studies in Chapel Hill, North Carolina, in the fall of 1973. The following summer, she developed and supervised the teaching of a curriculum in sex education for trainable retarded individuals. That fall she attended a three-day Program in Human Sexuality and Disability at the University of Minnesota medical school. The experiences confirmed her belief that she had found a career to her liking. She also worked as a consulting psychometrist in Mississippi and South Carolina during her time off from her studies, conducting evaluations of children with special problems. In 1975 and 1976, she did private counseling in the area of rehabilitation and sexuality in North Carolina.

Following completion of her doctoral studies at the University of North Carolina, she accepted a position as research associate at the Regional Rehabilitation Research Institute of George Washington University, in Washington, D.C. After fifteen months in that position, she was promoted to acting director of the RRRI, responsible for conducting and coordinating research and development, supervising research assistants, and preparing various reports for the Institute. Her major area of responsibility was as project director for the Sex & Disability Project, sponsored by the Rehabilitation Services Administration.

The project was one of the seminal efforts to study the need for rehabilitation professionals to become more familiar with the sexual adjustment needs of disabled clients. Susan and her colleagues found that more than 90 percent of disabled people responding to their survey indicated that they would actually take advantage of at least one of the twelve sex education/ counseling services listed in the survey form. Clearly, the interest was there among disabled individuals. Even more surprising, respondents checked an average of 4.4 of the 12 services, suggesting not only a desire for assistance but an interest in a wide range of services. By contrast, the same respondents rarely indicated having received such help in the past; they were in many instances deprived of essential information. To take just one example, almost half the respondents expressed interest in taking a course on sex and disability, yet only 2 percent had ever attended such a course. Similarly, while 40 percent wanted individual counseling, only 6 percent had ever had it.

Susan and her co-researchers also surveyed professionals in rehabilitation, discovering that the vast majority were not prepared to provide sex education and counseling services. This finding, together with the demonstrated need for such assistance among disabled people, was a deciding factor in Susan's next career move. Determined to meet the problem her research had brought to the surface, she accepted the position of head of the Department of Rehabilitation Counseling at Louisiana State University Medical Center. "I had sworn I would never return to New Orleans because of the deeply sexist nature of the professional and power systems here. However, I was offered a job I couldn't turn down: the opportunity to build, from the ground up, a whole new academic program in rehabilitation counseling. At the same time, I had grown restless in Washington. The work at GWU seemed dead once the Sex & Disability Project was completed, and the directorship of the institute required too much scrounging around for money and too much politicking. Here, I have a dean who scrounges for money."

She serves as head of the Department of Rehabilitation Counseling, School of Allied Health Professions, Louisiana State University Medical Center. It is, she says, the nation's only bachelor's degree program in rehabilitation counseling. In addition to her administrative responsibilities, she teaches several courses, conducts the thrice-yearly seminars, and serves a private caseload of rehabilitation clients.

IN HER OFFICE at LSU, Susan told me about an offer she had recently received to enroll in the university's medical school. She and the school's director of admissions both serve on the

medical center's committee that coordinates compliance with
section 504, the civil rights law for disabled persons. Susan
had told the admissions director of her problems years earlier
in attempting to gain admission to medical schools, including
LSU. The admissions head, a new appointee, had offered her
a chance to do it again. But by this time, Susan says, it was
too late. "I just can't do that any more. I can't sit through
class after class, keeping my mouth shut, and putting up with
the student-professor roles any more." But it was clear she
was pleased.

I asked her why she thought things had changed, and her
response was quick in coming: the law. Section 504 became
law in 1973 and took effect in 1977 with the issuance of regulations by what was then the Department of Health, Education,
and Welfare. LSU, like other colleges and universities, must
practice nondiscrimination in admissions and in other educational procedures. The law has resulted in searching reexamina-
tion by admissions officers throughout the nation of their
traditional belief that disabled people could not compete successfully in college. More and more, colleges are admitting
disabled students and are surprised to find that a large majority
prove successful.

But Susan also recognizes a more subtle factor. "The admissions director is a different man from the one who turned me
down cold back in 1970. The right people help a lot. It is
not just legislation and regulations."

It was the opportunity to teach that attracted her to the
medical center. "I love teaching and counseling and program
development. I especially enjoy the opportunity to work with
a limited number of people over an extended period of time,
helping them to learn what rehabilitation, disability, and sexuality are all about." She has found that brief, one-shot sessions
accomplish little more than sensitizing people to the overall
issues. In her classes, by contrast, she has several months to
expose her students to disability, to sexuality literature, and

to people with disabilities. One approach she especially likes
is a simulation exercise in which her students use a wheelchair
for an entire day, navigating the streets of New Orleans.

"One student really got into it once," she recalls. "After she
tried to enter a police station, a local television station caught
up with her. Soon she had a crowd, including reporters and
a camera crew, following her around town." Susan has found
that such experiences produce as many questions in her students' minds as answers. These questions then provide a spring-
board for discussion in class, leading to genuine growth in
awareness, sensitivity, and knowledge among her students.

In this process, students are forced to examine their own
motivations for entering the demanding field of rehabilitation
counseling. "I want my students to ask themselves: 'Why am
I doing this?'" Susan explains. "Too often, they give a vague
and superficial answer, saying that they want to help other
people. That's sometimes based on a lack of knowledge of the
field or a lack of knowledge about themselves. I tell them the
best answer is that rehab is fascinating. It's fun to be at the
front of a field during a period of innovation like this."

She believes her field is just beginning to understand what
it is all about. The enactment of section 504 and other laws
during the 1970s inaugurated an outpouring of interest among
disabled youth and adults in the possibilities for change in their
own lives. These individuals started with the experiences closest to their everyday lives, particularly rehabilitation itself.
They began to teach the very people who had been rehabilitating them just how demeaning and ineffective many traditional
rehabilitation practices were. And they began demanding
change.

"The past framework of rehabilitation is in a serious crisis,"
Susan told me in her office. "The national leaders lack vision.
I think they have stagnated. Basically, the whole field is floun-
dering; it would not be going too far to say that it is reactionary.
I feel the future is not going to flow from the past: there is

going to be a struggle, not a gentle passing. The two sides may be characterized in this way. On the one hand, we have the categorical, structured, now-in-control rehabilitation system of professionals giving services to what society sees—and maintains—as deviants. And on the other hand, we have an underground movement of people interested in social and professional normalization of the lives of disabled people, emerging leaders whose emphasis is not on 'treatment' but on 'adaptation' and 'options for life.' One will eventually squeeze the other out, both ideologically and fiscally. Almost every aspect of disability and rehabilitation work will be determined by this struggle. My great challenge is to help my students see the very real struggle and be prepared for the battle."

She sees sexuality as a central component of this struggle. The emerging leaders, unlike the old guard, recognize sexuality as a vitally important component of successful adjustment to independent living. These Young Turks are bringing the field of sexuality and disability into the mainstream of rehabilitation, insisting that the professionals providing services acknowledge the sexual nature of their clients and respond to the needs these sexual beings express. In this context, Susan notes that the Sex & Disability Project had found more than 70 percent of rehabilitation counselors to be untrained in the area of sex counseling. In large part for this reason, only one counselor in five reported initiating discussion about sexuality with disabled clients in an effort to determine whether counseling in this area was needed. Susan is determined to increase her profession's awareness of this responsibility to respond to the sexual needs of disabled people.

To accomplish this task, Susan is careful to define sexuality in all of its meanings. Drawing upon *Who Cares?*, she considers ten different meanings of the term. First, she says, sexuality is obviously a method of procreation. For many people, that is its defining characteristic. A second meaning is that it is a way of achieving spiritual union. Again, for many people, the religious symbolism and centrality of sexuality as a bonding force within marriage are primary. Sexuality can also be seen as a form of recreation; as a way to bolster one's ego; and as a way to release tension. All of these latter meanings relate to the emotional and physical aspects of sexuality. Sex can also be a form of communication and merging in which tenderness, concern, love, and affection are expressed; by contrast, sexuality can be a means to control and manipulate another person. Most people think of sexuality in one of these eight ways, although it can also be seen as gender identity and as activity of autonomic muscles culminating in orgasm. Trying to bring all of these different meanings together, Susan and her colleagues suggest that sexuality may be defined as the *integration* of physical, emotional, intellectual, and social aspects of an individual's personality which express maleness or femaleness.

In her work, Susan tries to help students recognize their own sexuality before they attempt to deal with the sexual needs of disabled individuals. This approach stems from Susan's own experiences: "My interest in sexuality came from my early ability in an all-Catholic high school and college to admit to and respond to the *fact* of adolescent sexuality." A similar recognition is required by her students, Susan believes, if they are to be effective. She stresses her belief that counseling severely disabled persons about sexuality is difficult enough for a well-adjusted counselor; for someone who has trouble coming to terms with his or her own sexual problems, the responsibility of providing psychological support and guidance for others is probably impossible. Susan favors positive and supportive responses from an experienced counselor. "The person who has an active encouragement response," she and her colleagues wrote in *Who Cares?,* "not only accepts the sexuality of disabled persons but also seeks to enhance sexual expression and fulfillment through direct intervention." She believes it would be the height of irresponsibility for a counselor to discourage a client, intentionally or through poor counseling, from giving full expression to these needs and desires.

These beliefs led her and her colleagues at George Washington University to list eight rights of disabled persons:

*The right to sexual expression. "No one has the right to limit the sexual expression of another person unless coercion, sexual use of children, or the high probability of an unwanted child (unwanted by the individual, not by society) are involved," they wrote in *Who Cares?*

*The right to privacy. They note that such rights are often violated in institutions, which is yet another argument against massive institutionalization of disabled persons.

*The right to be informed. All people need to understand their own needs, urges, and problems, and to learn about their opportunities and options so they can make reasoned decisions.

*The right to access to needed services. The authors of *Who Cares?* stress that access to general public programs on sexuality and to information made available to others is as important as, if not more important than, information and assistance specifically focused upon disability.

*The right to choose marital status. "No one has the right to decide for other adults whether or not they will be permitted to marry. . . . People also have the right not to marry," states the report.

*The right to have or not have children. "In our society," the authors note, "the decision to have or not have children is made by the potential parents. Disabled people are also entitled to this right. Information regarding genetic factors should be readily available to all people to determine the possibilities of passing on a genetic characteristic."

*The right to make decisions which affect one's life. "The right to make decisions implies the right to choose one's own values concerning sexuality," state the authors.

*The right to develop to one's full potential. "By receiving education and encouragement aimed at enhancing his or her sexual potential, a disabled individual achieves greater self-esteem, confidence, and independence. These changes may then influence the individual's perception of and motivation for other aspects of life, such as work, recreation, and community involvement. Rehabilitation, if it is to be truly meaningful, must address *all* aspects of a disabled person's life. Attempts to compartmentalize these aspects into narrow slots will only serve to undermine the rehabilitation process," they note.

The inclusion of the last two rights on this list reflects a conviction that sexuality is an integral component of what makes someone human, and that, therefore, professionals assisting or counseling disabled persons must respect the importance of sexuality to a person's overall development and growth in the rehabilitation process.

Susan stresses that special education and rehabilitation have in the past, but to some extent today as well, chosen to deemphasize sexuality. Residential and day schools for disabled children, for example, routinely have regulated dating behavior and have rigidly segregated students by sex. It is only in very recent years that any kind of sex education has been made available. Schools for disabled students were much later in adjusting to the special needs of pregnant teen-agers than were the regular public schools. It is as though the teachers and counselors did not want to recognize the fact that the students were sexual beings. This kind of official neglect, combined as it often was with severe punishment for any displays of sexuality, caused the students to suppress their sexual needs, to deny them, and to internalize the unspoken message that they were asexual neuters. Much like Susan in an all-Catholic high school, the students have been forced to turn to each other for comfort and for information.

As a result, many disabled adults are sexually confused and immature. Some are sexually maladjusted. The clients Susan sees express needs for the most basic kinds of sexual information. Susan finds, as do many other sex counselors working with disabled people, that the major problems are not adjustments to the particular physical requirements imposed by the disabilities so much as they are the difficulties of coming to terms with sexuality itself. The need to learn how to behave in a loving manner toward another person, without smothering the person in affection or controlling him or her out of jealousy or fear of rejection, is a basic one. So too is the need to recognize the powerful need each of us has for acceptance and love, and to learn how to deal with these feelings within the context of daily life.

Susan has found that many disabled persons were not given the kind of warm parental support they need to become well adjusted sexually as adults. For many parents, having a disabled child is a traumatic experience, one they often respond to by sending the child away from home to an institution or a residential school. On the child's infrequent visits home, the family becomes an entertainment committee, providing him or her with a false sense of what a family is and how to behave as a family member. Many disabled people have to learn that kind of role as adults, often from counselors experienced in helping them to make the transition from dependence in childhood to independence in adulthood.

Then, too, the whole question of contraception is a vital one for many disabled individuals. The fear of conceiving a child with a disability is probably stronger among many disabled persons than it is among others in our society, if only because the disabled individual is so keenly aware of the problems disabilities bring and because the individual suspects, or knows, that the disability had a genetic origin and may be inherited. Just as premarital pregnancy occurs most often today among relatively naïve teen-agers with little education, so too does the problem appear among many disabled individuals who just do not know how to prevent pregnancy.

Another problem Susan often encounters is the perception by some disabled individuals that they are too different to be attractive to others. This is often a particularly acute feeling among those disabled persons reared and schooled in regular settings, as opposed to special environments. Surrounded by "normal" youth, the disabled person is very conscious of the disability. Childhood and especially adolescence often are lonely and filled with a sense of rejection. Counseling to help the person come to see himself or herself as an attractive person occupies much of the time of the sex counselor, even when the problem presented by the client was originally one of a specific sexual nature.

And then there are the mechanical and physical questions. "Can I have sex if my legs won't listen to me?" is one common question, particularly among persons with cerebral palsy or other motor conditions. A deaf individual may wonder how to establish intimacy in a dark bedroom and how to know when the partner is asking for something to be done. The answers may be as simple as: "Leave the night light on" and "She will show you what she wants." A man or woman paralyzed from the waist down may need to learn to accept and enjoy oral or other kinds of sexual behavior, as well as identify additional erogenous zones.

Sex counselors sometimes do suggest different positions or strategies. Someone with limited sensation may need more than the usual amount of foreplay to become aroused. Similarly, a retarded individual may require explicit instruction by a sensitive individual who will take him step by step through the process of intercourse. Someone with a spinal cord injury may need to explore non-genital orgasm (many are surprised to discover that there is such a possibility). Sexual aids, devices, and techniques may be needed in specific instances, and instruction in their use offered. For example, vaginal lubricants may be needed because mental attitudes alone are not sufficient. Some individuals report increased sensitivity of the breasts, neck, ears, and lips following spinal cord injuries that decrease sensation in the genital area. It is even possible to "reassign" a sensation from a paralyzed area to another part of the body. Most spinal-cord-injured females are able to have successful coitus without unusual measures.

For women with spinal cord injuries or other severe motor limitations, positions other than the missionary may be preferable. For example, the woman may assume the top position, perhaps with pillows placed under her legs for support. Having the partners face each other may help limit unwanted leg movement as a result of spasticity. Rear entry, with both partners on their sides, may also help solve some of these problems. The partner having more mobility may assume the top position with arms and legs around the other partner, so as to control most of the movement that takes place during intercourse.

Some techniques that may enhance sexual satisfaction include breast stimulation, manual massage, mutual tellings of sexual fantasies, use of a vibrator, mutual masturbation, and use of oils or other lubricants.

Persons who are disabled may need to exercise special care in the use of contraceptives. The pill, for example, may cause blood vessels to clot or become inflamed. This has been found to occur with some able-bodied women, but it is believed to be more of a danger for a spinal-cord-injured female. If a woman uses an intrauterine device (IUD), her lack of sensation in the genital area may cause her to be unaware of mispositioning of the device and consequent damage to her body. Diaphragms may be difficult for a woman who has limited hand and arm control to place properly.

Males with spinal cord injuries may achieve and sustain an erection even though they have limited sensation in the genital area and are paralyzed from the waist down. Many may find it impossible to ejaculate, however, or to experience genital

orgasm. For these men, some of the same positions or procedures as are applicable for women may prove effective.

Susan has discussed some of these issues in her classes and
thrice-yearly seminars on sexuality and disability. Others she
has considered in articles and in book chapters she has contri-
buted, or in editorial work she has done for the journal *Sexuality and Disability*, which she serves as associate editor. She
is particularly interested in the psychological aspects of sexuality among disabled persons, stressing the need for mutual acceptance, understanding, and love.

In the hotly controversial field, her determined efforts to
promote recognition of the sexuality of people with disabilities
continue to encounter resistance from professionals who consider sexuality and disability to be mutually exclusive realms.
Susan believes, and I think she is right, that disabled people
will not be seen, nor will they see themselves, as truly equal
human beings until they feel comfortable about their sexual
problems and desires and can express them joyfully.

She relishes the challenge. Confronting sexuality head on
allows Susan to perceive and work on other attitudinal problems or perceptions her students and clients experience. It is
as though sexuality were a lightning rod attracting reactions
and responses, many of them revealing other issues which need
to be faced. Susan believes that this is just another indication
of the centrality of the issue of sexuality in rehabilitation.

It is central to her work, but it is not all-consuming. Susan
still swims regularly, as she has most of her life for therapeutic
reasons, but now it is for enjoyment. She loves to cook, read,
and travel, particularly to New York City to visit museums
and see Broadway plays. Living with her in her home eight
miles from the medical center is a young Brazilian woman
she sponsored in this country who has muscular dystrophy.
And she gets together regularly with close friends of both sexes.

Of her relationships with men, she treasures most the growth
opportunities each has afforded her. "While most of my friends

51167
WITHDRAWN

3291

LEE H. S. LIBRARY - BAYTOWN, TX.

were falling in love and getting married, I was falling in love
and not getting married. And yet I'm not sorry I got involved,
nor do I regret any of the moments, some sweet to remember,
others probably best forgotten. Each time I enter into a relationship, whether it is a sexual one or not, I find a new aspect
of myself more clearly defined and articulated. The finding
out is worth it."

Looking back on her romances, both short and long, she
finds them expressions of a life style she has created for herself.
"When I'm lonely or afraid, I see my life style as a failure to
realize a close, caring primary relationship. I may even indulge
myself in a good session of self-pity. Then the pendulum swings
and I see that all lives, mine especially, are a matter of compromise and each way has its own joys and aches. I've done it
my way, and I have no regrets."

On her first thirty-two years, Susan waxes philosophical. "My
question is not 'Why me?' but 'What next?' There is no answer
to the first question. Nobody knows why certain people are
born disabled. But 'What next?' asks the question: 'What are
you going to do with the rest of your life?' And that is something
I can do something about."

3

ROBERT SMITHDAS

"Death never had a stillness like this one that I know."

ONLY ONE PERSON has surpassed the remarkable record of achievement of the celebrated Helen Keller. That man is Robert Joseph Smithdas, fifty-five, the first deaf-blind person to earn an advanced degree. Now director of community relations for the Helen Keller National Center for Deaf-Blind Youths and Adults in Sands Point, Long Island, New York, he is happily married, a proud home owner, and a fiercely competitive fisherman.

Bob's accomplishments would be distinguished enough for someone with full use of all his senses. He is an honors graduate of St. John's University, holds a master's degree from New York University, and has received three honorary doctorates. He has written two books and delivered more than three thousand lectures to some two million people throughout the United States and much of the rest of the world. His schedule leaves little time for avocations, yet he has become so expressive a poet as to earn the Poetry Society of America's Poet of the Year Award.

What he calls the "silent fog" has deprived him of sight and sound since the summer of 1930, when he was a strapping five-year-old in depression-ravaged Pittsburgh. People who are deaf learn by making maximum use of their sight; through lip-reading, reading, and sign language, they try to acquire what others learn by hearing. Conversely, people who are blind sharpen their auditory skills, seeking to obtain by listening information most people acquire through their eyes. But for Bob Smithdas, and thousands of other deaf-blind people, both of the lead senses are forever closed.

Bob has expressed his profound losses in many ways, but never so vividly as in his deeply felt poem "Silence":

> There never was a silence
> as deep as this one is:
> a silence filled with circling thoughts
> and spanless distances.

Death never had a stillness
like this one that I know,
where space and time stand idle
and my brain rocks to and fro!

It should not be surprising, then, to find Walter Cronkite
calling him "superhuman" or Barbara Walters saying that he
is "the man who has made the most lasting impression of my
eleven years of interviewing." Anyone who has overcome such
an unimaginable stillness so completely deserves every honor
he can get.

How refreshing to discover that he wears his laurels so lightly,
a quiet, unassuming gentleman genuinely eager to meet new
people and help others solve their problems. The impression
one receives upon meeting Bob is that he is a man at peace
with himself. He seems to have accepted, and adjusted to, his
dual disabilities, content with the senses of taste, smell, and
touch and the world they reveal to him. He smiles easily and
frequently, giving no evidence at all that the fires of determination and ambition still burn.

That is not altogether a false image. Yet Bob harbors deeply
felt passions and firmly held beliefs, convictions and emotions
that guide his life and shape his poetry: about the value of
human life, the nobility of exquisite phrasing, the joy of independent living, the tenderness of a moment completely experienced, and the power of the senses he has forever lost. It is
not anger, he is not an angry man, but it is sorrow; not bitterness, but poignancy; not detachment, but a powerful involvement. If something matters to him, it matters intensely. Having
struggled so long and so hard to live his life, Bob is fully, irrevo-
cably, and finally committed to life, the bad with the good,
the pain with the joy, the frustrations with the victories.

As director of community relations for the Helen Keller National Center for Deaf-Blind Youths and Adults, Bob is responsible for developing and conducting public-awareness campaigns
to increase the general understanding of deaf-blindness and
of the center's ability to help deaf-blind people. Bob spends

a great deal of time in public-speaking engagements, delivering more than two hundred speeches annually. He writes and edits a nationally distributed newsletter describing the center and its programs. From time to time, he appears before congressional committees to testify on legislation. It was as a witness before one such committee in 1967 that he helped secure enactment of the law establishing the center itself. He participates in senior staff meetings of center personnel involved in educational, vocational, and other endeavors, assisting them where needed to garner community support for their work. And he works individually, often informally, with deaf-blind youths and adults who live and study at the center, offering them a role model, an example, an inspiration, and often just an encouraging word.

Watching Bob in these activities, one notices how quickly and unobtrusively his sign language interpreter keeps up with the conversation in meetings and conferences. Bob places his hands on the interpreter's, following the signs and finger spelling with ease. When he talks, Bob uses his own voice. To take notes, he makes indentations in Braille with a pin and special paper. Bob uses a teletypewriter (TTY) device converted to Braille when he needs the telephone. The device produces Braille versions of what the caller types; it is a modified form of the one many deaf people use to communicate with each other. To talk with persons not equipped with such a machine, Bob relies upon his interpreter as he does in meetings, feeling the message in his hands and responding with his own voice. He is also skilled at one-to-one communication without an interpreter, placing his hands gently on the other person's lips and throat to "lip-read" and replying in normal speech.

Each of these methods of communication had to be learned in long, often tedious, sessions over a period of years. He has had to struggle mightily to keep his speech intelligible; five decades of deafness have trained him to use kinesthetic cues to feel what he cannot hear and thus to monitor the volume and pitch of his speech. Lip-reading by touch, too, is extraordinarily difficult. Bob brings to it fingers attuned to minute sensations from years of reading Braille. To sign and read sign language, he has had to visualize, somehow, the movement of hands in space and memorize the meaning of each motion.

I first met Bob at a conference on deafness in March of 1973, in Williamsburg, Virginia. As he was waiting to check in at the hotel, I introduced myself to him, placing my hands in his, letting him feel my signs and finger spelling. Bob's rejoinder surprised me. Not only were his signing and spelling fluent, but his facial expressions were far more mobile and animated than I had expected. Bob and I had no difficulty at all comparing notes about the speeches we were scheduled to give, about our flights to Williamsburg, or about our mutual friends. Much of that initial ten-minute conversation has remained with me in the years since. But it was the sense of easy calm that most impressed me, possibly because as a deaf individual I am especially sensitive to visual cues.

I have often wondered about that calm. That Bob Smithdas has strong emotions cannot be doubted by anyone with even a passing familiarity with his poetry; certainly "Silence" could not have been written by anyone other than a person seared by the pain of intense loss. Yet those feelings are for the most part masked in interpersonal communication. That he is ambitious is evident from his accomplishments and his steadfast refusal to admit that he cannot do something; yet, again, unless one spends a lot of time with Bob and comes to know him well, that ambition is not evident.

Why, then, the calm? Over the years, several possible explanations have occurred to me. My knowledge of many blind people suggests that Bob, like numerous others who cannot see, has gradually adapted to a life that requires almost incessant waiting: for someone to enter and speak to him, for something to be said which reveals how his words have gone over. For Bob, this adjustment to blindness and the need to wait must have been compounded by the additional burden of un-hearing ears. When one can neither see nor hear others, a great deal of time is spent in imposed isolation, a removal from stimulation that itself acts to produce the appearance of patience.

Then, too, the same factors must lead Bob to withhold full expression of his emotions until he has an accurate understanding of the other person's feelings. Uncertainty about how friendly or interested the other is suggests that the most appropriate posture is one of cautious openness and, again, patient waiting. Consider, for example, how often each of us ventures a noncontroversial remark upon first meeting another person, and how carefully we couch expressions of opinions, looking repeatedly at the person to whom we are talking to catch any disagreement early enough to change our remarks, retract our statement, and avoid embarrassment. As a deaf-blind person, Bob misses both the body cues, such as facial expressions and posture, and the vocal intonations, including pitch and other inflections signaling skepticism, sarcasm, or ridicule. That he is careful in what he says until he knows someone very well should not be surprising.

But as I came to know Bob better, three considerations seemed more convincing as explanations for the serenity which attracted and baffled me. None has to do with his disabilities. First, Bob is in an environment which he knows extremely well and which makes him very comfortable. He has worked for the Industrial Home for the Blind, sponsor of the Helen Keller National Center for Deaf-Blind Youths and Adults, since 1952. During these twenty-nine years, he has performed a variety of public relations, community relations, and program coordination tasks which suit his talents and interests. A natural outgrowth of performing work at which one is highly competent and long experienced is exactly the kind of serenity Bob exudes. The second consideration is related to the first: Bob has done and experienced almost everything he can expect to encounter in the course of a normal day. Incidents which earlier generated high excitement or deep anger now elicit milder responses as a natural product of the maturity that comes with wide experience. And third, Bob has accomplished about everything an individual can reasonably expect to achieve: he has every reason to be satisfied, content, and, yes, serene.

For all of this, Bob has passionate convictions. Perhaps the most powerful is that symbolized by his own life: deaf-blind people can achieve and live lives of meaning and dignity. This belief is his preoccupation, the driving force behind his life. Bob devoted two full decades to an unrelenting effort to overcome deaf-blindness. For the next thirty years, he worked with several thousand other deaf-blind individuals, helping them to surmount the loneliness and isolation of deaf-blindness. He has spent, then, half a century doing everything he knows how—writing, lecturing, composing poetry, counseling, and showing by personal example—to get across the point that deaf-blind people can be helped to live productive, useful lives. He has given his life to a belief, and not many of us do that.

Another of his passions is a love of language, a delight in precision and expressiveness, a joy in the use of language to evoke memories and visions he has no other way of sharing. To appreciate Bob's love affair with English, one needs to recognize how long the odds against his mastering even rudimentary language became when he lost his hearing early in life. For most people deafened in childhood, a fifth-grade reading level is an achievement. But Bob Smithdas made an important discovery early in his education: the key to his success over deafness and blindness would be mastery of language, for it was that key which would unlock specialized knowledge he would need and open the doors to vocational success. As he began to understand the complexities of English, he quickly fell in love with its endless intricacies, its ability to go beyond utilitarian uses to express uniquely personal and beautiful visions and thoughts. A lifelong fascination with poetry resulted. Bob's intense dedication to unraveling the mysteries of language has given him all the control over English he needed to succeed in his education and in his career. But it has given him more. It is this pursuit—the never-ending quest for just the right word or phrase—that excites him still, that keeps him young, alert, curious, and always seeking more.

Just as he has sought to overcome deaf-blindness and to master English, so too has he worked ceaselessly to become as completely independent as humanly possible. For a child or an adult who is deaf-blind, few things are more natural than responsiveness to external stimulation, guidance, and direction. It is only too easy to become dependent upon others, to permit them to do for you what you have not yet learned to do for yourself, and to allow them to shape your life and each of your days. From earliest childhood, Bob has been a person who rebels against such control, a boy and then a man who thrives on taking his own risks and pursuing his own challenges. That passion still drives him today. It is that desire to do it himself that leads Bob to own his house, do his own repairs, and even hang his own wallpaper; the satisfaction of knowing that he did it and did it well.

In recent years, Bob has broadened his vision considerably. Content in the knowledge that he had achieved independence in his own life, he felt ready, at last, to assume responsibility for the life of another. Bob was nearly fifty when he married the former Michelle Craig, a deaf woman who had lost her sight in a snowmobile accident. She has filled his life with energy and excitement as no one else had before, her effervescence banishing forever the loneliness that Bob knew as his constant companion for almost half a century.

And he has grown increasingly insistent that others who are deaf-blind have the ability to achieve what he did and deserve the chance to try. Bob is not content, if he ever was, with being a token, an exception, a superachiever. But more and more, he is calling upon his colleagues in services to deaf-blind people to employ, consult, and listen to persons who themselves are deaf and blind. He takes great pride in the knowledge that he is the first person since Helen Keller to complete a college education. But he is determined not to be the last.

THE DISEASE that was to have such a devastating and pervasive effect on Robert Smithdas's life struck without warning one summer afternoon in 1930, as he awoke from a nap at the family's home on Sunnyland Street in Pittsburgh, Pennsylvania. He remembers feeling a sharp, stabbing pain in his lower back—and then nothing. Regaining consciousness three months later, he discovered that he could see only "a thick, muddy fog," and that he had lost all hearing in his left ear. He was soon to lose his hearing in the other ear as well. The disease had a name he did not recognize, meningitis.

A five-year-old is just beginning to make sense of the world around him. He knows what school is, but has not yet attended one. He knows a little of reading and writing, just enough to appreciate how much he does not yet know. And he faces each new day with excitement, eager to see new sights and hear new sounds. He accepts these senses, vision and hearing, as natural; he literally cannot imagine life without them.

So it was for Bobby Smithdas. He did not appreciate the beauty of spring mornings, the brilliant hues of a rainbow, or the thousand other views he had seen until he could no longer see them. Nor did he relish the sounds of rain and thunder, the stirrings of music, or other sounds quite so much as when he could no longer hear them. These are the gifts deaf-blindness takes away immediately, and they are mourned passionately. What is more important to the child's ability to live a life, the contribution made by hearing and vision to keeping him in communication with people around him, is less understood at the beginning but more missed later. And missed terribly: the great curse of deaf-blindness is not that you cannot see beautiful art or hear lovely music, but rather that you are cut off from your fellow human being. You are alone.

Bob has described deaf-blindness as a "silent fog" and the isolation it brings as akin to sailing in a fog-enshrouded ocean without a compass or rudder. He remembers the first six months of deaf-blindness as having been especially frightening. In his 1958 autobiography, *Life at My Fingertips*, he recalls being:

> unable to distinguish between night and day except by the vibratory movements of the people around me, the warmth of the sun on my face. Time had no meaning. Life was simply a continuous physical rhythm. . . . It is a curious fact that when I finally learned to distinguish between day and night, I developed an acute fear of darkness. It is difficult to explain why I should have been afraid of the dark when I could not see it. Yet, whenever the warmth of the sun left my face, and I realized night was coming on, I would cling to anyone who happened to be at hand.

The five-year-old Bobby Smithdas had three senses remaining—touch, smell, and taste. He used all three, plus the little remaining hearing in his right ear, in a voracious, inexorable quest to understand his world. Climbing into the attic, rumbling through closets, tasting every item in the kitchen, and even the flowers in the garden, he banished his fear of the unknown by turning it into a known. Around his home, he learned to identify his position by the smell of the trees, grass, and flowers. In the neighborhood, his clues were the shapes of the terraces and hedges. Even in a vacant lot, apparently devoid of directional cues, he was able to orient himself with tufts of grass, the slant or rise of the ground, and the texture of shrubbery.

It may well have been this insatiable curiosity that saved Bobby Smithdas. Certainly, had he been passive rather than active, waiting for the world to come to him, he would have developed much more slowly. A child who lacks reliable hear-

ing and vision is without exactly those senses that bring information into the mind, that stimulate thought, and that provoke
reaction to what is happening around him. The child with normal hearing and vision can afford a certain amount of relaxed
passivity; indeed, the amount of information coming in through
the eyes and ears may occasionally be overwhelming, and withdrawal from it necessary from time to time. But a deaf-blind
child like Bobby Smithdas must generate information himself,
must seek it out, and must comprehend it without the advantages of sight and hearing.

Bobby "listened" to music, feeling the beat and rhythm of
the melodies and sensing the difference between drums, horns,
and harmonicas through touch more than through hearing.
Gradually but surely, the hearing that remained in the right
ear was leaving. Others in his family would shout directly into
his ear, repeating again and again until he understood; as time
went on, even this did not produce comprehension.

Now, even his driving curiosity was not enough. Bobby
needed, desperately, a reliable way to communicate with others, to learn more than could be acquired through touch, smell,
and taste. And he knew this, remembering life with hearing
and sight. So when a Miss Clare at the Western Pennsylvania
School for the Blind in Pittsburgh introduced Bobby to Braille,
he attacked the system with single-minded devotion: "I kept
practicing until the tip of my forefinger grew numb and the
skin was worn through." He absorbed the manual alphabet
and American sign language as fast as his teachers could instruct
him, driving himself mercilessly to master what he knew would
be the tools that would at last unlock the larger world he had
left behind when meningitis struck that warm summer afternoon.

Bobby's rapid progress soon outpaced Western Pennsylvania's capacities to assist him. He was the only deaf-blind child
enrolled in the school. His teachers were not trained to meet
his special needs, nor were his classmates receptive to his over-

tures of friendship. "My habit of feeling and smelling everything irritated them," he recalled. "They gave me the nick-
name Smearcase." As a result of the school's limitations, Bobby
was slipping behind his classmates. His speech was deteriorat-
ing rapidly because his hearing was no longer adequate to monitor it and because his teachers were not trained as speech
therapists. Nor could they help him understand them, knowing
little or nothing about lip-reading and other techniques to help
deaf children.

The solution—the only one, it seemed at the time—was a
transfer to the Perkins Institute in Watertown, Massachusetts.
Perkins, unlike the Western Pennsylvania School, was equipped to teach deaf-blind children and in fact had already enrolled several his age. Bobby moved to the institute in the
middle of the fifth grade, living away from home for most of
the year. But it was worth it: at Perkins, Bobby regained his
sadly diminished self-confidence. His mother and father knew
that Perkins was his last best chance. Just before seeing him
off to Watertown, his mother said to him: "Bobby, you will
never have a chance like this again." As it turned out, he would
need only this one.

Bobby's well-developed senses of taste, touch, and smell were
stimulated as never before by the carefully designed
campus at Perkins. As he later recalled: "It has been a principle with the founders of Perkins that the unseeing and
unhearing should live in an aesthetically inspiring environment, for beauty has its own channels of communication even when the senses are deficient." Years later, the experience of walking around the campus remained with him: "After a few weeks of bloom, the blossoms fell, covering the ground
with a muffled carpet. And when I walked along the flagstone
paths of the herb garden, my footsteps crushed the leaves of
thyme and sorrel, sending up a curtain of tart, mingled fra-
grances that hung in the air like a giant censer." This sensitivity
in touch, smell, and taste struck me as remarkable. I wondered
whether he was aware that most people with normal hearing

and vision rarely realize that their senses are capable of picking up such detailed information about their environments. He nodded sadly. "I know. But what makes me even more despondent is the knowledge that they do not appreciate the senses I have lost. Seeing and hearing are so much more powerful than the senses I have, and yet I don't think most people appreciate them." He has expressed his longing for these lost senses in several poems. One I like particularly is "Light," a four-stanza poem. These are the first and fourth:

> Once my eyes were filled with light
> and the glory of the sun and stars and moon,
> and all the world of radiant colors
> were mine without asking. They flowed
> into my consciousness every morning
> like the flood tide of the sea
> suffusing every nook of my being.
> I used to stand by my window
> and watch the red yolk of a rising sun
> spread out into a blaze of gold
> over the green treetops. In the evening
> I would see its fire sink down behind the hills
> until it burned itself out
> in the silent ashes of night.
> . . . . . .
> But all this was long ago
> when I was a child and could not understand.
> The gift of light was always there
> shining in through the windows of my eyes
> and I accepted it without question
> because it was such a natural quality of life.
> But having lost its glory forever
> my memory clings to its preciousness
> tenaciously. And sometimes in my dreams
> the distance of thirty years of darkness is drowned
> in the river of timelessness
> and I find it once again.

Bobby learned to sense changes in weather by the weight of the air against his face. As he later described it: "The air at night is heavier than during the day and the fragrance of the night world is more clearly defined to my nostrils. If I had not been violating the conventional timetable, I would have much preferred to do my living in the evening and sleep all day. When the earth is hushed, senses are much more alive. The night winds are the master music makers of the skies." This admission is as revealing of the change brought about at Perkins as any other, because it shows how much Bobby had adjusted to deaf-blindness and how much he had learned to take full advantage of the senses left him. The five-year-old terrified of the night he could not see was forever gone now, never to return.

During his first few years at Perkins, Bobby further developed his finger spelling and signing skills while picking up a new way to communicate: lip-reading. The technique depends upon extremely sensitive fingers, which Bobby by this time had because of his constant work at Braille. By placing his thumb over another person's lips, with his other fingers resting gently on the throat, Bob is able to understand normal conversational speech. "Lip-reading opened up an entirely new world of communication for me," he would later recall. "For the first time, I was able to appreciate with my fingers the changing relationships of the voice and facial expression. I learned, for instance, that anger is a very generalized emotion: the voice becomes harsher and often rises in pitch; the mouth tightens; the head invariably thrusts forward; and the body becomes more rigid in posture." He was able to glean all of this merely by touch.

But the method, called the Tadoma approach, had its limits. On cold days, for example, his fingers would be too insensitive for him to follow conversations. Then, too, success in lip-reading varied with the individual, with some people much easier to follow than others. He found it easier to read women than men, and southerners than northerners, usually because of the greater vibration in the throat when women speak and the tendency of southerners to form words farther in front of the mouth than do others.

He also made an astonishing discovery: people smile in different ways. He found that people whose smiles naturally curl the mouth upward tend to be happier than those whose smiles seem more horizontally made. And, by trying out the different kinds of smiles, he found that he could affect his own mood.

His progress in reading Braille, in lip-reading, and in finger spelling and sign language enabled him to absorb, for the first time, the full range of academic information presented by his teachers in the classroom. He literally could not learn enough. Bob's excitement at discovering biology and chemistry, mathematics and physics was great. But he fell in love with words. It was English he loved best, where he found his passions overflowing, and where he felt himself compelled to go beyond what was offered in the classroom to explore the original writings of hundreds of authors, especially poets.

Bob particularly liked the Romantic poets, Shelley, Keats, and Wordsworth, for their direct imagery and use of simple but apt words. A. E. Housman and Robert Browning he detested because of their use of "quaint language." His visit to the home of Henry Wadsworth Longfellow in Cambridge, Massachusetts, was a highlight of his years at Perkins. Bob had been writing his own verses as early as the third grade, but now, after exposure to the Romantic poets, he spent more and more hours writing his poetry.

As a change from the discipline of study and writing, Bob decided to try out for the wrestling team. Although Perkins had long fielded a team of blind wrestlers, Bob received little encouragement. "Are you crazy?" asked one of his friends. "No deaf-blind person has ever succeeded in becoming a wrestler." But one member of the team taught him the fundamentals and the coach gave him a chance to try out for the team. Bob's approach to this opportunity was typical: he drove himself mercilessly. As he recalled much later:

> Although my elbows and knees became painfully abraded from my continual mauling on the heavy cotton cover of the mat, I refused to concede that my case was hopeless. Gradually I

learned how to defend myself against nelsons, the cradle, and
the figure-four scissors. I practiced running on the circular track,
punching the bag, exercising with pulleys, and lifting weights.
I did finger tip pushups and situps. Slowly my reflexes became
more rapid; I developed an instinctive muscular balance, an
intuitive sense which told me when an opponent was shifting
to a new hold. I learned to block on the defensive; studied all
the methods used by others in making their opening attacks.
My sense of touch became keener, my balance and posture improved as I learned to control my muscles at will.

After one full year of such preparations, he was crestfallen to
be eliminated in the tryouts for the team during his sophomore
year. So he spent another full year exercising and practicing.
The following fall, he made the team.

It may seem remarkable for someone to spend two years
trying to make a school wrestling team, but this was typical
of the way Bob lived his life. Others might have given up,
but he could not allow himself the luxury of admitting defeat
without first being absolutely certain that he had made his
best and last effort. Characteristically, he wrestled for his team
despite illness, injury, and cuts. Bob likes a saying that expresses
his approach to such challenges: "The Chinese have a proverb
that says, 'The journey of a thousand miles begins with a single
step.' "

Following graduation from Perkins in 1945, Bob entered
the Industrial Home for the Blind in Brooklyn, New York, for
vocational training. He learned to wind brooms, fold tape, and
sew, performing work contracted to the Home by various governmental agencies participating in the war effort. He proved
so skilled in manual labor that he set records for production.
This left him largely unmoved. But what did stimulate and
challenge him was the awesome task of learning to walk the
streets alone.

He mastered the use of a cane easily enough. It was crossing
streets that terrified him. Once he was almost robbed by a
man who helped him across; another time he enraged a woman

who volunteered to help him, only to be ignored because Bob could not hear her. Despite crashing into fences and sustaining numerous bruises from falls, he eventually gained courage and experience. It was at that point that the Home decided to teach him to navigate New York's labyrinthine subway system.

The trick, he learned, was to ask a passenger at each of the transfer points to guide him to the track for the next leg of his journey. Bob carried a stack of cards, each of which he was to show to some passenger in order to be led to the correct spot. On his first trip, he showed it inadvertently to a blind individual, who, of course, led him to the wrong platform.

Early in 1946, Bob was ready to make a try at his long-time ambition: to go to college. He was inspired by the example of Helen Keller, but was painfully aware that she was the only deaf-blind person to have been graduated from a college. With the support of the Home staff, he decided to attend St. John's University in Brooklyn. Financial assistance was arranged from the New York State Vocational Rehabilitation Service, the American Foundation for the Blind, the Howe Memorial Fund, and the Home. Bob spent several months training a nineteen-year-old, Johnny Spainer, to serve as his attendant and interpreter. While he was teaching sign language and Braille to Spainer, the Home arranged for his textbooks for the freshman year to be transcribed into Braille.

Just before classes started in September, he achieved a life-long goal, to meet Helen Keller. As he recalls that first meeting:

> Miss Keller took my hand in her own. I remember vividly how warm, how energetic, her handclasp was. She was then in her sixty-fifth year, but no one would have guessed it if he had merely taken her hand. Her eager clasp conveyed all that youthful vigor which has characterized her personality and set aside the weight of years. "I think it is wonderful that you are going to college, Bob. It has been nearly half a century since I graduated from Radcliffe, and times have changed so much since then. You have courage to begin a project like this. You will have many difficult situations to face. God knows the trials you will have to endure.

But you will succeed, I am sure of it. You will overcome all the difficulties if you really believe in yourself."

That brief conversation has stayed with Bob for thirty-five years as one of the highlights of his life.

He would need all the inspiration he could get. With Johnny translating lectures and taking notes as well as Brailling these notes after classes, Bob settled into an intensive routine of reading bulky Braille volumes and memorizing information from lectures and texts. Often, he would study all night. "Burning the midnight oil is an understatement," he recalled. "I would burn away the whole night without sleep. I studied in half-hour periods; then I would sit still, holding my head in one hand while I tapped off the information I needed with the fingers of the other." When he took tests, someone would read off the questions for Bob in signs and finger spelling, and Bob would type out his answers. To prevent distraction for other students, he arranged to take the tests in a private room.

But it was not all drudgery. Bob was thrilled to be initiated into Sigma Tau Alpha fraternity and to attend the frat's parties, which provided him with his first dates.

In the summer before his junior year at St. John's, Bob took courses in rehabilitation of the blind at the University of Michigan. The six-week session in Ypsilanti was unforgettable for one reason: blue-eyed, brown-haired Betty. For the first time in his life, Bob Smithdas was in love. The dinners, long walks, dances, and endless conversations of that love affair still bring smiles to his face. Betty was seriously interested in marriage, a prospect that filled Bob with a hitherto rare emotion: an overwhelming sense of inadequacy. He felt unable to assure her of any stability and support for the rest of her life, and resisted all entreaties to the contrary. Eventually, the affair ended; Betty later married and raised several children in suburban Ohio. For many years after that 1948 romance, Bob wondered if ever again he would meet a woman about whom he felt so strongly—and whether someday he would feel confident of himself as a husband, father, and breadwinner.

In fact, it would be twenty-six more years before he felt ready.

His last two years at St. John's were filled with intensive study. A bus accident in the winter of 1949 took him away from his classes for two months, making success even more elusive. Two lengthy term papers had to be redone; they were blank because he had forgotten to put a ribbon in the typewriter. His final semester was made especially difficult by the necessity of taking two extra courses in order to qualify for graduation.

But he made it. Having appeared on every term's honors list, he was graduated *cum laude,* in the upper 10 percent of his class at St. John's, in the spring of 1950. He was the first deaf-blind man ever to get a B.A.

Bob immediately made plans to go one step further. He enrolled at New York University that fall for a master's degree in rehabilitation in order to prepare for a career of helping blind and other disabled persons. Once again, it was a first: no other deaf-blind person, male or female, had ever received an M.A. His comment about receiving the diploma is characteristic: "It pleased me, of course, to know that I was the first deaf-blind person ever to progress so far academically; and it satisfied me even more to realize that now that the way to higher education had been demonstrated, others like me would follow my path and undoubtedly go even further."

The Industrial Home for the Blind immediately hired him as a public relations specialist. His job was to crisscross the country delivering lectures to business groups, civic associations, and organizations of professional workers in rehabilitation about deaf-blindness and the Home's programs. His preparation for this assignment was typically thorough. For fifteen years after losing his hearing in both ears, Bob had worked constantly to maintain his speech. Now he trained intensively under the direction of a professional singer who was also blind, John di Francesco. Bob considered it the most thorough immersion in speech instruction he had ever experienced. But he was soon to learn that there was more to the fine art of speechmaking.

Bob's first attempt at the effort revealed one unforeseen problem. Johnny Spainer, still his aide, tried to explain it as gently as he could. "Bob, you turned a little too much to the right. You kept moving gradually toward your right—just a little at a time. When you finished you were completely turned away from your audience." Simple adjustments, such as use of a podium or table with which Bob could orient himself, were made. Johnny would sit beside him, using a system of hand signals to indicate that Bob should raise or lower his voice and to cue him on the time left before he had to conclude his talk.

Bob learned almost as much from these lectures as did his audiences. He was constantly amazed by how little the general public knew about blindness and deafness. The same questions would come up again and again. Can blind people really work and support themselves? How do they read? Can deaf people learn to talk? These kinds of inquiries redoubled his determination to speak to as many audiences as possible. He once estimated that in a typical year he delivered 250 speeches to 112,000 people.

Gradually, he began to become involved in other activities as well. He served as a consultant to the World Council for the Welfare of the Blind, a United Nations–associated organization, to establish an international system of communication for deaf-blind individuals. For four years, from 1957 to 1960, he conducted research on new approaches to rehabilitation of deaf-blind persons. By 1962, Bob's experience was sufficiently broad to merit his promotion to associate director of the Home, in charge of its deaf-blind department. During these years, he continued his public speaking, now appearing before as many as a quarter of a million people each year.

He was selected as Handicapped American of the Year for 1965. At the ceremony, held April 28, 1966, Hubert Humphrey presented the award on behalf of President Johnson. That same year, the Taplinger Publishing Company printed his volume of poetry, *City of the Heart*. Stories about his work appeared in the *New York Times*, the New York *Daily News*, and the Washington *Post*.

Even while celebrating his successes, Bob continued to drive for greater personal independence. One of his proudest accomplishments was moving from the residential facility he had lived in for many years to his own apartment. As he later recalled, "A home meant many things for me: a measure of personal independence in not being bound to the regulated life I had hitherto known; the reassurance that I could make my own decisions without criticism from others. But perhaps more than any other reason, it offered a new challenge to my ingenuity and resourcefulness. Would I be able to maintain a home and resolve all the problems it might entail because of my disabilities? Would I be able to solve the usual problems of domestic housekeeping—cooking, cleaning, buying supplies for an apartment—and act as a host when friends came to visit?"

The apartment was on the eleventh of twelve floors. For the first few days, he found himself getting off on the wrong floors. Cooking was a major problem because he had never before prepared meals for himself. But these and countless other problems were solved, one by one, with ingenuity and help from his colleagues and friends from the Home. A continuing problem was locating items; he had to remember where he had placed each one or spend lengthy periods searching the entire apartment.

So that he could be alerted to the ringing of the doorbell, he asked a friend to attach the bell to an electric fan, which would generate a slight breeze he would feel. This worked only if he was sitting or standing near the fan. He soon learned to make arrangements with friends to time their visits and to leave the door unlocked at those times. Gradually, he solved these and many other daily problems. The feeling of privacy, relaxation, and independence was, he remembers, worth every agonized moment he had to endure along the way to self-sufficiency.

Yet with this new excitement at being able to live by himself came another, less welcome, companion: a deeper sense of loneliness. "Loneliness is a hunger for increasing human companionship, a need to be part of the activity that I know is constantly going on about me," he has written in his autobiography, *Life at My Fingertips*. "To share moments of joy with someone else, to have others sympathize with my failures, appreciate my accomplishments, understand my moods and value my intelligence—these are the essential conditions that are needed for happiness."

Partly to relieve his anxieties, he threw himself into the activities of the Industrial Home for the Blind with greater vigor. As associate director in charge of services for deaf-blind clients, he found that he constantly had to think beyond his own needs and desires. He planned numerous events, including Christmas-Hanukkah parties and Helen Keller dinners, at the Home for the eighty deaf-blind clients in his department. One evening each week, he organized recreational programs and games for the clients. From time to time, he helped them shop, visit the doctor, and solve domestic problems. He even made tools and other equipment for his clients in the Home's workshops.

The 1963 epidemic of German measles, or rubella, resulted in thousands of deaf and deaf-blind infants, many with other physical and mental disabilities. Bob knew that these children would soon need services at centers like the Home—and that their numbers would greatly exceed the Home's capacity. He began to insist, first at professional meetings and later on the lecture circuit, that a new center would soon be needed to meet the needs of these people. In 1967, he testified, along with Dr. Peter Salmon of the Home, before Congress on behalf of a new national center for deaf-blind persons. A few months later, the National Center for Deaf-Blind Youths and Adults was established by law.

The center began operation in 1969 in a converted, cramped warehouse in New Hyde Park on Long Island, New York. Capacity was limited to eighteen persons; a staff of twenty was hired. It was not until 1973 that construction of a new campus was completed, the number of trainees was increased, and the present staff complement was obtained. Five years later, by act of Congress, the center was renamed the Helen Keller National Center for Deaf-Blind Youths and Adults.

By this time, Bob was director of community relations of the center. His work included public speaking, radio and television appearances, presentations at professional conferences, and preparation of brochures and other written material on the center and its programs. He appeared on the NBC *Today* show, on *The Ed Sullivan Show*, and on numerous other nationally broadcast programs. And his public speaking engagements took him to forty-five states.

And then something new and very different happened to Bob Smithdas. As he recounted it to me, the beginning was modest enough. "In 1971, I received a letter from a young woman in Golden, Colorado, asking about services of the center. She had just lost her sight due to a snowmobile accident during her senior year at Gallaudet College, the national college for deaf people. Despite her blindness, she had learned Braille quickly and continued courses at local colleges in Denver. Her name was Michelle Craig."

Bob responded to her immediately. "It was obvious to me after reading her letter that she needed encouragement. I suggested that the center could be of assistance to her by providing training. An exchange of letters followed, and finally a date was set for her admission. By an odd fluke of circumstance, on the day that Michelle arrived at the center, I was walking in the hall when I was stopped by one of our counselors and introduced to Michelle, who had just come into the building.

"It is difficult to explain the sudden, overwhelming interest I felt in this young woman as soon as I met her—at the time, I thought it was merely a wave of sympathy, perhaps compassion. She had extremely poor balance, seemed so unsure of herself, yet had a vivacious, outgoing spirit that captivated me. From the first day, we seemed to gravitate to each other, spending lunch periods and coffee breaks together."

I myself had met Michelle at Gallaudet, before she lost her sight. We met again at New York University in 1973, when she attempted to pursue a master's degree at the Washington Square campus. Despite the university's attempts to provide her with the kinds of assistance she needed, it was apparent to her and to her counselors that she needed more training in independent living and adjustment to deaf-blindness before she could cope with the stresses of the city and the university.

I told Bob that Michelle had impressed me, too, with her remarkable openness and curiosity. "I guess she was vulnerable, Bob."

He agreed, but said that he had sensed much, much more in her. "Marriage never entered my mind in the beginning. In fact, I had always said that I would never marry a deaf-blind woman! But as time passed, the relationship between Michelle and myself grew deeper and more intense. Gradually we realized that we needed each other and finally we began planning for our marriage."

The reaction to news of the pending wedding caused precisely the opposite reaction among his peers from that Bob had encountered a quarter of a century earlier with Betty. Then, he had resisted countless pleas to go ahead with marriage. But now, he told me, "When we announced that we planned to marry, it caused consternation at the center. Other directors rushed to tell me that I might be making a mistake. Even Dr. Salmon, who had been my mentor for years, seemed concerned."

But this was a different Smithdas. No longer fearful of inadequacy, he now had no doubts about his ability to be a good husband and to provide for a wife. He was also steadfast in his conviction that Michelle was the woman he wanted to marry. "Gradually, Dr. Salmon and the others came to realize it was not a spur-of-the-moment relationship or a passing whim," he recalled. They decided to go ahead with their plans.

On December 13, 1975, precisely at noon, Father Rudy Gawlik, who had been close to Michelle at Gallaudet, celebrated a wedding Mass for Michelle Craig and Robert Smithdas at St. Edward the Confessor Church in Syosset, New York.

Soon, the new couple bought their own home in Port Washington, near the Helen Keller Center. Bob describes it as "a charming house, but like all houses it has had its problems—plumbing and electrical failures and all that. Whenever possible, I do most of the repairs myself, but sometimes there are emergencies that require professional workmen." With a grin, he added: "Friends told me that it was not possible for me to do certain remodeling chores in a house. Despite their misgivings, I papered our kitchen walls and put in a new tile floor in the large downstairs family room. I have been told since that both jobs look professional and friends find it hard to believe that the work was done wholly by myself."

The awards kept coming in. Gallaudet awarded him an honorary doctorate of letters. From the University of Western Michigan, he received an honorary doctorate of humanities. Then, in January, 1980, his alma mater, St. John's University, gave him a doctorate of humane letters. "Because I have such vivid, heartwarming memories of my undergraduate days at St. John's," he told me, "this honor has very special meaning for me."

TODAY, after more than five years of marriage, Bob feels more content and more relaxed than at any time in the past half century. But his pace has barely slackened. In addition to serving on the President's Committee on Employment of the Handicapped, he continues to work for the World Council for the Welfare of the Blind of the United Nations, acting as the chairman of its committee on services for the deaf-blind. For three years, he was on the Architectural and Transportation Barriers Compliance Board's advisory committee in Washington, D.C., and he has also served in recent years on other committees, including the council of the National Conference of the Disabled and Disadvantaged.

He has been the guest of the Ministry of Education in Japan and has traveled to Holland and West Germany. In part because of these international activities and in part because of his deep desire to improve services in the United States, Bob participated actively in the International Year of Disabled Persons (1981), sponsored by the United Nations.

The "silent fog" remains as impenetrable as it ever was, but Robert Joseph Smithdas has seen and heard more than most of us can ever know.

4

ROGER MEYERS

"Getting married is like coming out of retardation."

ROGER MEYERS WORKS as a busboy in Love's Restaurant, in El Cajon, California. Because of the recession and continuing inflation, Love's is only able to employ him one day each week. To supplement his earnings, Roger depends on a Social Security program called Supplemental Security Income (SSI) as well as a Department of Housing and Urban Development program of rent subsidies. He and his wife Virginia are eligible for these programs because of their retardation and because their income from other sources falls below federally established minimums. Roger remembers his problems retaining eligibility when he was working four days a week at Love's and was offered an additional day's employment. The extra income would have made him ineligible for SSI benefits. It is something that troubles him deeply.

Roger's problems were on my mind as I worked to reform the legislation authorizing the SSI program. We wanted to make it possible for disabled individuals like Roger who wanted extra work to be able to get it without jeopardizing their benefits from the program. So when President Carter signed the 1980 reform bill eliminating many of the "work disincentives" from SSI, I called Roger immediately to be sure he knew about it.

As I always did with Roger when we talked about the complex SSI legislation, I built up the subject carefully and spoke slowly. And as he always did, he surprised me with his quick grasp of what I was saying.

"Roger, remember you were telling me about working Friday nights at the restaurant? About how you wished you could work more?"

"Yeah, right. If I earn too much, they take away the SSI that pays the rent, the phone, and the food."

"Well, Roger, maybe soon you can work more. There's been a change in the law. I think it will take effect October first.

What the change says is that people who get SSI assistance can work more without losing benefits."

"They changed the law? Hey, great. I've been saying they ought to, you know. I've been thinking that if they don't, in ten years, twenty years, the rent and everything will go up and I don't know how I will take care of Virginia."

I wanted to caution him that the changes in the law would not necessarily mean that more work would be offered to him. The law does not say that SSI beneficiaries must be given additional employment; it is not a jobs-creation bill. Rather, the effect of the bill is that if additional work is available, a beneficiary may accept some or all of it without losing eligibility for the program. But I didn't want to confuse Roger, so I stuck with the immediate subject at hand.

"Now, Roger, I'm not sure how the change in the law will affect you. You have a counselor, don't you? What is her name? Nancy?"

"We don't have a counselor any more. We have a psychiatric social worker. That's Nancy. She's coming over tomorrow."

"Why don't you ask her, Roger, to find out about this for you? Tell her they've changed the law and you want to know if you can earn more, and if so, how much more, before losing your benefits. Here, if you have a pencil and paper, I'll give you the numbers that identify the law. You can tell Nancy which law you're talking about."

After he located a pencil and took down the bill's number, we talked a bit more. "I'd really like to work more. Like I said, inflation is making everything more expensive. It will help a lot if I can make some more money. The rent just went up, like it does every year, and Virginia and I were just talking about how we would pay it."

"Let me know how it works out with Nancy, Roger."

"O.K. Thanks. Bye."

There is little exceptional about this conversation—unless you know that Roger Meyers is retarded.

In the span of just ten minutes, he had shown an ability to plan ahead as much as a decade or two, an appreciation of the economic factors affecting his life, a keen sense of what is in his best interests, and a voter's desire to change laws to meet his needs more adequately. Implicit, as well, in this talk are the facts that he is married, a wage earner, a resident of a private apartment he and his wife maintain without live-in help, and a self-sufficient individual who receives only occasional counseling to help him with special problems.

Roger's intelligence has been assessed a number of times, with IQ scores on these tests ranging from a low of fifty-eight to a high of seventy-five. The intelligence quotient is a scaled score, with one hundred representing average intelligence. A score of fifty-eight means that Roger's intelligence is at the lower end of the mild retardation range, while seventy-five places him in the borderline retarded range. Such fluctuations are not uncommon among retarded individuals; taken alone, they mean relatively little. What we can say with confidence is that Roger is mildly to moderately retarded.

Retardation is understood today to indicate not just a score on a Stanford-Binet test of intelligence, but also a certain level of functioning. The currently used definition of retardation, adopted by the American Association on Mental Deficiency, recognizes a combination of factors, including the test score and social adjustment as well as the age at which the condition is believed to have begun. Most retarded individuals, more than three in four, are mildly retarded. The more severe conditions are much more rare.

Mild retardation means different things for Roger depending upon what he is trying to do. His social intelligence—that is, his ability to function smoothly in day-to-day routine activities—is much higher than his academic or conceptual intelligence. He has, for example, learned how to conduct most of his usual financial affairs, including paying the rent, buying groceries, and the like. He also understands and adheres to the unwritten rules of social conduct that regulate our interaction with other people. Similarly, he remembers most of the critical events of his own life and can describe these in detail, even when the incidents occurred several decades in the past.

On the other hand, Roger has real difficulty conceptualizing abstract ideas. He has a hard time understanding how to plan for his future. While on one level he knows that inflation is increasing the prices of most items he buys, he does not know why this is so, nor does he understand how he can combat inflation. The concept of purchasing things on credit in order to pay for them in "inflated dollars" as opposed to buying in cash is one he would have great difficulty comprehending. While many of us can see that we are ahead of the game paying 12 percent interest on an item purchased on credit during a period of 15 percent inflation, and accordingly believe that the item actually costs less when bought over time, this is not something Roger can appreciate without extraordinary effort.

Similarly, he can use numbers he encounters in his everyday life, but with important limits. He knows how much he must pay for rent, for example, and can compute what a 10 percent increase in rent might mean. In this case, he would move the decimal to the left one space in order to represent what 10 percent would be. But for anything requiring more complex calculations, say a 15 percent increase in rent, he cannot compute the increase himself and must rely upon someone to tell him. To take another example, he often talked with me about the SSI limit on earnings, which at the time involved a figure of $2,250.00. Roger writes this out as $2000, 200, 50. He needs to separate the components of the figure in order to understand it. A third example: Roger does not understand why a two-liter bottle of soda costs more at a small convenience store than at a large supermarket. He will recognize that the difference in cost exists, and take advantage of it, but he will not realize the relationship between market factors of supply and demand as they affect the pricing policies of businesses.

Roger is acutely aware of his limitations. And he is determined to rise above them. He talks often of "growing out of retardation." It is for him a consuming ambition. He sees that others around him know more than he does, and he relates that fact to their lack of retardation. His conclusion: by learning more, he will lift himself out of retardation.

While he continues this effort, Roger experiences a sense of uneasiness about what he does not know. It would not be too strong to say that this is a fear of the unknown. Because the future is, of course, unknown, Roger sometimes fears it. This came out when we talked about the change in the SSI legislation. Roger frankly does not know how he is supposed to deal with inflation and is deeply fearful of what rising expenses might do to him and to his wife, Virginia. Related to this is a difficulty in thinking ahead. Roger finds it much easier to remember what has happened to him than to envision what is likely to happen to him. The past is known, frozen, understood; the future, by contrast, is unknown, shifting, and defies understanding.

The birth defect that is believed to have caused Roger's retardation also affected his fine-muscle control. Roger continues to have difficulty with his hands. When he writes with a pen, for example, he grasps it with his full palm, wrapping the fingers around it, and presses down on the paper firmly. On his notes to me are indentations in the page deep enough for me to feel them easily; that is how hard he presses down when he writes. Similarly, when he drinks a cup of coffee or lifts a spoon to his mouth, he must concentrate intently upon keeping his hand steady, to avoid spilling anything because of the spasmodic movements of his arm.

And Roger is highly sensitive about the word "retardation." It represents what Roger wants to eliminate from his life: it stands for what he does not like about himself. When I sent him a paper I had written, in which I noted that he was retarded, he crossed out the word and substituted "exceptional."

This word, a favorite of special-education administrators, is a broad one covering not only disability but also children who are gifted and talented. To be retarded, for Roger, is to be "slow"; to be exceptional is just to be different in some rather vague way.

Roger symbolizes for me the difficult issues involved in two of the most agonizing battles I fought during my tenure as ACCD director. One was reform of the SSI system so that people like Roger, who wanted to work but could not at the time even afford to try, would be able to take a chance on employment. For more than two years, ACCD tried to make the case for increasing allowable earnings of beneficiaries as a "work incentive" that would in fact save the government money. Just as we were making real progress in this effort, the federal government tied to the pending legislation language that slashed the benefits to be paid to future beneficiaries. All our efforts to disentangle these statutes were in vain. Thus, the bill passed by Congress and signed by President Carter accomplished much that was good, particularly the removal of "work disincentives," but much that was harmful as well.

The provisions of H.R. 3236, as the bill was known during consideration in the U.S. House of Representatives, were so very complex that I found them impossible to understand without translating the statutory language into highly specific effects on particular individuals. One person I thought of often during this period was Roger Meyers. His intense desire to work and his deep anger at what he considered unfair limits to the amount of work he was allowed were never far from my mind. Thus, during the first few months after the Carter administration introduced the language that eventually became law, I was vigorously lobbying on the Hill for enactment of these vital changes. Even after the negative implications of other parts of the bill became clear, and our support for the measure fell sharply, I continued to seek enactment of these work incentive provisions.

The other battle in which I often looked to Roger for inspiration and instruction was the long effort to expedite de-institutionalization of retarded individuals who are not in need of constant hospitalization. Begun when several retarded residents of Pennhurst Center, a massive institution outside Philadelphia, brought suit against Pennhurst, the suit traveled through the district and appeals courts and the Supreme Court before being decided. ACCD became involved as an organization supporting the retarded plaintiffs and their families early in the effort. The horrors made public during the course of this legal proceeding reaffirmed my determination to help as many people as possible receive the relatively normal upbringing Roger had experienced. There was no doubt in my mind, from the moment I first read the Washington *Post* story by Roger's brother Robert Meyers about the family's attempts to deal with his problems, that Roger Meyers would not be anything close to the independent, self-sufficient individual he is today if his parents had been forced to place him in an institution.

The Pennhurst legal struggle was exasperating because the defendants persisted in appealing the case despite the fact that they had not even offered a defense on the district court level. The Pennhurst superintendent himself told the district court judge that "there should not be a Pennhurst." Yet community fears about "dumping" of retarded individuals apparently compelled the defendants to appeal. The opposition to the plaintiffs' contentions, then, was political—not legal, educational, psychological, or medical—at the most basic level. In my frequent talks with the lawyers handling the case for the retarded plaintiffs, this fact kept emerging; how, we wondered, could we fight this if, even though we had all of the critical factual evidence on our side, the decision kept eluding our grasp? How many possible Rogers would lose their last best chance for a real life while the lawyers dickered over yet another delay?

In the years since Robert Meyers's 1977 *Post* series, I have come to respect Roger Meyers tremendously. In his own quiet way, he is an enormously determined man who absolutely refuses to permit himself the luxury of accepting his mental limits. He *will not* be retarded.

He has told me about his "studies" in mathematics, history, language arts, music, dancing, and arts and crafts. When I ask him about his day, these are the first things he mentions, an indication of their importance to him, particularly because he is not permitted to work more than a few hours a week. Roger uses library books, a blackboard in the apartment, and notebooks to teach himself what he does not yet know. He believes that after sustained study, over perhaps twenty years, he will know enough to be no longer retarded.

But it is about his job that he comes alive in conversation, describing with real pride the work he performs at the restaurant. His duties at the bar in Love's are to remove dishes and glasses from tables after customers have finished, reset the tables with place mats and utensils, and bring water and menus for new customers. I once asked him how he liked the activities he had taken up since learning that he would not be able to work as much as he had liked. It took him a few moments to respond: clearly, nothing can replace work as a source of pride and joy in achieving despite his limitations.

I risk making Roger sound rather droningly dull in his persistence toward his goal of becoming non-retarded. But while it is true that this determination dominates his life, at least as far as I have come to see, it is also true that he has learned to enjoy each day as it comes. He talks with delight about watching horror movies, for example. ("I saw the scary one, what was the name, Virginia, oh yes, *The Exorcist*," he said on one occasion. On another: "We watched a *Godzilla* movie. She was more afraid than I was. I liked the monster best.") He and Virginia are avid TV viewers, subscribing to Home Box Office for first-run movies without commercials. When I asked him which regular television programs he liked best, he rattled off the names quickly: *Barnaby Jones, Charlie's Angels, The Flintstones,* and *Popeye.* On occasion, for fun, he will form Virginia's ponytails for her ("I make for her two ponytails with two rubber bands on a certain type of wire. Sometimes it makes her mad!"). He also likes to go fishing. One time, after we had talked about his fishing adventures, I told him that he sounded remarkably like one of my neighbors, and he laughed, pleased. I did not have to mention, of course, that my neighbor was not retarded.

And he still remembers his excitement when his brother Robert's book, *Like Normal People,* based on the *Post* series, was made into an ABC-TV movie. *Like Normal People* was published by McGraw-Hill in hardcover and by the New American Library in paperback. Telling me about the movie, he could not resist a gentle gibe at his wife: "I was excited, but Virginia was more nervous than I was. Mostly, Virginia's mom was nervous." The life of a celebrity, however brief, appealed to him. With relish, he talked about the party at the home of the program's producer in Los Angeles and about the party a few nights later at Love's Restaurant. "I had forgotten they were going to show it that night, but the people at Love's didn't. It was real crowded and a lot of people watched it at the bar," he told me. It is clear that he values the affection of his colleagues and customers at the restaurant and that the party was important to him.

And he is valuable to them. His boss from time to time has offered him additional hours, work he has had to decline to date because of the restrictions in SSI legislation. Another indication of his importance to the restaurant is its tolerance for his need to escape for a while when he feels more pressure than he can take. At times, he will disappear into the men's room for as long as an hour to calm himself down. Such behavior might result in dismissal for a less important worker. His colleagues at Love's, however, have learned to follow him and tell him to come back out "because we need you." Says one waitress: "He makes this place run."

There is a well-known psychological concept that explains the tolerance of his co-workers. Called the competency/deviance hypothesis, it holds that persons who have demonstrated competence and importance to others are permitted greater degrees of deviance before being called to account for such quirks of behavior. As Robert Meyers shows in *Like Normal People*, Roger's value to the restaurant during the busy Friday evening hours he works is such that colleagues are willing to permit his unusual expressions of his feelings, much as many people permitted Bobby Fischer his erratic and often eccentric actions because of his demonstrated genius at chess.

Roger's excursions in search of solitude probably emerge from a lifetime of loneliness. For most of his life he has been with non-retarded individuals, many of whom rejected him as a peer, and so he has grown accustomed to being alone much of the time. Whereas others might react to intense frustration by striking out in aggressive behavior, Roger will withdraw into his customary solitude.

Such deviations are much more rare today than they were in the past, particularly since his marriage to Virginia. His family, friends, and colleagues marvel at how much he has grown and matured in the three years he has been married. He and Virginia support and reinforce each other. When I asked him if he and his wife fight as much as most married couples do, his immediate answer was that they argue "when I forget something, or Virginia forgets. We remind each other about things, and sometimes we get angry at each other." Just as withdrawal during times of stress is not unique to Roger, nor an expression of retardation, Roger's quarrels with his wife are normal and routine, another small indication of their maturity and growth.

Indeed, there is amazingly little about Roger's life today that is markedly different from those of millions of other thirty-three-year-old men with families. He has emerged from decades of excruciating work to learn what so many of us pick up effortlessly. His problems, and he does still have problems, are relatively minor ones compared with those he has faced successfully in the past.

That fact strikes me as enormously important: many—indeed, most—retarded people have much more potential than they are usually given credit for. As tragic as this is, it pales before the unspeakable cruelty of denying retarded individuals even the minimum of human consideration and assistance, warehousing them into massive institutions that merely keep them alive to breathe another day. The Pennhurst case history is filled with stories of individuals with as much potential as Roger who never will reach even a small fraction of his achievements. The counsel for the plaintiffs in this litigation, Thomas K. Gilhool of the Public Interest Law Center of Philadelphia, assembled a painstaking display illustrating just what insensitive treatment can do to people like Roger. The record indicates, and here I am quoting from the codified opinion of District Court Judge James Broderick at 446 F. Supp. 1295, United States District Court for the Eastern District of Pennsylvania, 1978, *Halderman* v. *Pennhurst State School and Hospital:*

> The average resident age at Pennhurst is 36, and the average stay at the institution is 21 years. Forty-three percent of the residents have had no family contact within the last three years. Seventy-four percent of the residents are severely to profoundly retarded. The average resident has had one psychological evaluation every three years and one vocational adjustment service report every 10 years. Those residents who have had more than one Vineland examination (measuring social quotient) during their residency at the institution have, on the basis of this test, shown a decline rather than an increase in social skills while at Pennhurst. . . . Pennhurst is almost totally impersonal. Its residents have no privacy—they sleep in large overcrowded wards, spend their waking hours together in large day rooms

and eat in a large group setting. . . . No psychologists are on duty at Pennhurst at night or over the weekend, thus, if a resident has an emotional crisis, he or she may go without treatment until the next morning or until the weekend is over. Moreover, routine housekeeping services are not available during evenings and weekends, thus it is not uncommon to find urine and feces on ward floors during this period.

Broderick goes on to illustrate that educational programming for the benefit of the residents averaged less than fifteen minutes per day. Only one out of every six residents with a hearing impairment had been treated or fitted with a hearing aid; of three hundred nonverbal residents in need of communication training, only twenty-two were being served. Broderick also demonstrated that physical restraints were used far too often as a means of controlling the residents. One resident was in a physical restraint for more than 650 hours a month for three straight months, with therapy to help her not even begun until four months later. More than half the residents were on psychotropic drugs, an extraordinarily high proportion; equally serious, physicians monitored the effects of these drugs on fewer than one out of three affected residents. Broderick continued:

> Most toilet areas do not have towels, soap, or toilet paper, and the bathroom facilities are often filthy and in a state of disrepair. Obnoxious odors and excessive noise permeate the atmosphere at Pennhurst. Moreover, the noise level in the day rooms is often so high that many residents simply stop speaking. . . . In addition, there is some staff abuse of residents. In 1976, one resident was raped by a staff person; one resident was badly bruised when a staff person hit him with a set of keys; another resident was thrown several feet across a room by a staff person; and one resident was hit by a staff person with a shackle belt. . . . Terri Lee Halderman, the original plaintiff in this action, was admitted to Pennhurst in 1966 when she was twelve years of age. During her eleven years at Pennhurst, as a result of attacks and accidents, she has lost several teeth and suffered a fractured jaw, fractured fingers, a fractured toe, and numerous lacerations, cuts, scratches, and bites. Prior to her admission

to Pennhurst, Terri Lee could say "dadda," "mamma," "noynoy" (no), "baba" (goodbye), and "nana" (grandmother). She no longer speaks.

Pennhurst has improved in many respects since these incidents occurred; it has also taken appropriate disciplinary action against staff members who maltreat residents. The striking fact about Pennhurst that helps to interpret all of these data is that Pennsylvania is recognized as one of the nation's best states in providing residential care for retarded individuals; if Pennhurst offered so little to its residents, one can only speculate on the level of care available elsewhere.

Roger Meyers's parents were repeatedly advised to place Roger in an institution, advice they steadfastly rejected. The one place they were regularly told to send Roger was Willowbrook, the institution made infamous by Geraldo Rivera's television documentary in 1972. Robert and Roslyn Meyers cannot recall exactly why they rejected the advice of so many doctors during the 1950s, but some need, perhaps their continued hope that they could help Roger better than an institution could, compelled them to keep him close to home.

Had they followed the advice of the best physicians they could find, there is little doubt that Roger would not be living in an apartment today. He would still be in the institution, and he would not remotely be the Roger he is now.

Yet, and this is important, had they done so, their own lives likely would have been different. Helping Roger through his childhood, adolescence, and early adulthood took a great deal out of Robert and Roslyn Meyers, and placed great demands upon Roger's brother Robert. That they had to suffer so much, for what was unquestionably the right decision, speaks volumes about society's attitudes toward retarded individuals, then and now.

I OFTEN ASKED ROGER about his background but there were significant limits to how much I could learn from him. Fortunately, his brother Robert permitted me to draw upon *Like Normal People* for much of this important material. For the full story of Roger's childhood and early adulthood, I refer the reader to that book.

Roger Drake Meyers was born August 8, 1948, to Roslyn and Robert T. Meyers of Kew Gardens, Queens County, New York. The birth, at five minutes before midnight, was uneventful in itself, with no complications, although two days earlier Mrs. Meyers had been taken to the hospital for a false labor. The Meyerses still do not know exactly what caused Roger's retardation, but they suspect that oxygen deprivation through a break in the amniotic sac enveloping the fetus at the time of the false labor may have been the cause.

Roger remained at Kew Gardens General Hospital for almost two weeks before coming to the family's apartment one mile away. Soon after, his crib was placed in the room of his brother Robert, five years older. Within months, Roslyn and Robert Meyers began harboring suspicions that "something was wrong" with their infant son. Comparisons between Roger's development and Robert's earlier progress through the first stages of infancy revealed disturbing deviations: lethargy, erratic swings of mood and behavior, head drooping, lack of response to stimulation. These were at first dismissed as the normal differences between babies, but as time went on it became increasingly difficult for the parents to explain away Roger's actions.

As the baby's maternal grandmother repeatedly raised questions, Roslyn and Robert Meyers were forced to ask themselves an awful question: was Roger retarded?

Recalling these first months of Roger's life, Robert suggested in *Like Normal People* that his parents' sustained refusal to admit that Roger might be mentally deficient was one of the shaping factors in his brother's life: "To deny it was to fly in the face of observation, and yet that denial is one of the reasons Roger has developed into the person he is. By denying to themselves and others that he was retarded, they unconsciously and indirectly set out to prove that he was *not* retarded and so gave him as many experiences as a non-retarded person would get. That is just what the experts recommend today."

It was then that the visits to physicians began. Because I went through a similar series of endless trips and because my parents received almost the same kinds of bewildering advice, I can understand what the Meyerses went through during these early 1950s years. But I doubt anyone who has not experienced this frustration will comprehend the utter confusion, deep hurt, and anger Roslyn and Robert Meyers knew.

They began the visits with the unexpressed and feared knowledge that it was likely that Roger was retarded. They sought and yet avoided confirmation of this suspicion. Just to make the first trips took great courage. To continue took more: they could not get an answer.

Roger was "diagnosed" as having a wide range of disabilities, each with its own diversity of treatments. One week, the problem was a hearing loss: buy a hearing aid. The next week, it was a speech impediment: send him for lessons. Then it was retardation: warehouse him in an institution. Once retardation was confirmed as Roger's problem, the recommendation became almost unanimous: institutionalization.

It was a common recommendation, not only for retardation but for other severe disabilities. My parents remember being told to send me to a "state school" because of my deafness. "It was what they were told, Frank," my mother told me. "The doctors were taught very little about disabilities in medical school. Some were told almost nothing. When it came to disabilities they could not cure or treat well, they were taught to refer the child to an institution. What is frightening, and what worried us when you were a child, is that most of these doctors had never even been to the places they were recommending we send you." The same fears haunted the Meyerses.

Robert remembers his mother's fury at yet another professional telling her to institutionalize Roger: " 'That got me so mad I just can't tell you. After all my work with him, all of our efforts to teach him to read, to groom himself and be sociable, to be told to send Roger to one of those places where he'd be ignored or harassed or sexually abused—never!' "

Roger's father's anger was equally bitter. As Robert tells it, his father became sarcastic in his views of the advice he was getting: " 'One of these clowns told us to be happy that Roger lived in the age of electronics, so he could get all his information about the world from television, because he would never learn to read or write. Another man told us to "warehouse" him immediately, that there was no hope for him. Somebody else suggested a new surgical procedure, just going on in Switzerland, which might find out what the problem was—even though the operation had a high fatality factor.' "

Institutions represented just about the only ongoing programs for retarded individuals at the time. During the 1950s and early 1960s, their populations grew steadily as more and more retarded individuals, products of the World War II baby boom, were referred—and stayed, for decades. The institution played several critical roles for society, despite all the horrors associated with its abuse as a treatment approach. First, it sheltered society from those who were different: it got "those people" off the streets, out of sight and out of mind. For many citizens, and indeed for many parents unable or unwilling to cope any longer with the strain of raising a retarded child, that was exactly what was needed. And second, it brought together in one place people with common problems, making it much more convenient for doctors and other specialists. The argument was made, and few ventured so far as to verify it, that such places were "in the best interests of the child."

The Meyerses rejected institutionalization. What to accept proved a difficult decision. In their neighborhood in Queens, and throughout New York City as a whole, very little was available that would meet Roger's needs. Roslyn worked day and night teaching him everything she could, getting him ready for the school she hoped someday to find. He learned to dress himself, to listen attentively to others, to answer simple questions when called upon. Throughout it all, Roslyn continued searching for educational programs. She found classes for retarded children but was appalled to discover that they were more baby-sitting operations than educational sessions. Eventually, when he was five, she placed him in a nongraded, integrated setting at the Queens School, a private cooperative school a short distance from the family's apartment building.

The stimulation at the school was just what Roger needed to spurt ahead in his development. His teachers were sympathetic and gave him individualized attention. Academically, he blossomed. Socially, it was another matter: being constantly around non-retarded children and forced to compete with them made Roger increasingly nervous. It was then that he began "going into the bathroom" when the frustration became too much for him. After school, he would come home and spend long periods in his room, grateful to be left alone for a while.

He was at the Queens School for five years. During that period, his intense concentration and drive to achieve and, yes, to excel, became more and more pronounced. Talking with Roger's teachers much later, Robert was told again and again: " 'He tried so hard, he really did.' " And he knew he was trying harder than the others, yet falling more and more behind them. Roger did not understand that, so he became increasingly frustrated. I myself can identify with all of this: the academic stimulation of school (being away from mother-teacher!), the loneliness among nondisabled children, the feeling that never really leaves you that you have to keep trying, and the hurt and bewilderment at seeing yourself behind the others without knowing why. It was not until I was a teenager that I realized the relationship between not hearing and not learning things other children picked up automatically.

Roger was twenty-one before he understood that he was retarded. By that time, of course, the drive to achieve was well
established, together with the anxiety formed from years of
unexplained failure. My peers in school thought of me as "bull-
headed." Robert said something similar about his brother:
"Roger has always been like that, even as a kid—stubborn as
the morning, not giving in."

While Roslyn was working with Roger and seeking help for
him, Roger's father was plunging into his work as a salesman
and sales executive with a drug company. He hoped to make
a "financial killing" that would enable him to provide for Roger
for life, even after he and Roslyn were gone. It became a preoccupation, even an obsession, for Robert T. Meyers. He would
"'get some equity,'" he told his son Robert, money that he
believed would relieve the family of much of its anxiety. In
pursuit of his goal, he worked endless hours, often weekends,
gradually building up his reputation and, with it, his salary.
As another step toward protection for Roger and for the family,
he took out massive life insurance policies. But the search for
"some equity" was unsuccessful: Robert never made the financial killing he so desperately wanted.

While he tried, the burden of raising Roger fell largely to
Roslyn. Robert T. would help on weekends and in the evenings.
Together, they sought to give Roger the same kinds of life
experiences his older brother received. At that time, there
was no word for what they were doing—indeed, professionals
rarely understood the importance of it enough to consider nam-
ing it—but much later, a term emerged: integration into the
life of the community. Another, broader term expressing not
only these trips and activities but a whole philosophy of care
for retarded individuals came into use in the 1970s following
experimentation in Denmark and Sweden: normalization. The
concept today is to provide retarded individuals with as normal
an upbringing as possible, in every conceivable way, so as to
stimulate them to grow and develop as much they can. But

in the early 1950s, normalization was still far in the future. The Meyerses were following their instincts and relying upon their experiences with their older son.

Roger was never hidden from the neighbors or from the extended family of aunts, uncles, and grandparents. That was important in helping others around him accept him as a member of a family, not as more different from than like other people. Yet it also produced its stresses on Roger. During these years, and in fact until his marriage, loneliness was Roger's most constant companion. And it placed a large burden on his brother as well. Robert remembers feeling less like a brother than like a second father, feeling responsible for taking care of as well as playing with Roger. So completely did he play that role of surrogate father that Roger called him "Dad" for a while before coming to know him as "Bobby." This is all part of the price, it seems, of raising a severely disabled child at home.

Even in these early childhood years, while he was still at the Queens School, Roger demonstrated the intense determination and single-minded devotion to achievement that was to characterize him for so many years to come. It was almost as though he believed that through sheer force of will he could make himself become as "good" as the other children, gain their acceptance and respect, and escape the never-relenting fear of inferiority. Looking at Roger's life from the perspective of hindsight, now that he is in his thirties, one can make a very good case for the claim that he has in fact done that: he has succeeded. Retardation is not a constant, unchanging fact of life so much as it is a function of how the individual copes with the daily challenges and frustration he or she faces. Roger has come to learn how to do many things thought to be beyond someone with his mental capacity—to do long division, for example, and to make change. There is no other explanation for this than to recognize that he lifted himself by will power, if not out of retardation altogether, then surely out of the lower levels of functioning that were expected of him.

As *Like Normal People* shows, it was seldom easy for him. For much of his life, he has had a speech impediment which made it very difficult for people who didn't know him well to understand what he was saying. Such difficulties are common among retarded individuals. Typically, he refused to admit that his speech would remain imperfect. John Pelzer, the school's maintenance man at the time, told Robert that he remembered Roger's determination to speak: " 'Roger always knew what he wanted to say, but because of his speech impediment, he'd stutter and get frustrated. His face would turn all white and he'd shake his hands in sheer frustration. But he didn't let it stop him. No sir, he'd go up to a new child here, and he'd say, "What's your name?" just like that.' "

And he was teased mercilessly by the other children. Roger had great difficulty realizing that people might try to take advantage of him or ridicule him because of his problems. Rather, he would think of the harassment as something he just went through, and often, in fact, something he actually enjoyed because of the attention it brought him. Still, there were many times when he would come home from school in tears and be unwilling or unable to talk about his frustration for days to come.

Strikingly, Roger remained unaware of the fact that he was retarded. Certainly, his parents never forced him to comprehend or accept his limits. Throughout the Queens School period, and for years thereafter, Roslyn and Robert Meyers would continue to deny that Roger was retarded. They would talk about a possible new approach in language therapy or speech therapy, they would seize upon rumors of a new drug or surgical procedure, and they would talk about Roger "snapping out of it" someday, as though that might really happen and end the nightmare forever.

Roger's lack of knowledge about his condition must have made the daily frustrations extremely difficult to understand, accept, and cope with. His classmates would do better than he, and he was not able to understand why. The only solution appeared to be to try still harder. And that is what he did.

One wonders whether his parents were right to withhold from Roger the fact of his retardation. It is easy to understand why they did. After all, they continued to hold out hope that it would all be "cleared up" someday soon, so why worry the child unduly? And then, too, there was the concern that Roger might use the fact of a disability as an excuse, a crutch, a reason for giving up. It is all too easy to do that. On the other hand, Roger was struggling mightily to do what was, objectively speaking, an impossible task: he was trying to become what he was not and never would be.

Looking back, Roger's parents insist that they did tell him. And it is likely that they did, at least in part, but that he did not understand it at the time. When Roger learned of his retardation at the age of twenty-one, perhaps it was as much the fact that he was old enough and mature enough to understand what was being said as that the message itself was clearer and more definite than it had been in the past. So it would seem that the parents did what they could and what was right: they tried to tell him in an honest and gentle manner about his condition, in terms he could understand at the time, yet held out hope of eventual cures, insisting enough upon them that he came to view the problems as temporary, not as the serious ones they in fact were.

In 1956, the family moved to a larger apartment in Queens. Robert Meyers had taken a new position in the advertising business and wanted to give his family the benefit of his higher earnings. Despite the move, the tensions that accompanied the family's attempts to cope with Roger's retardation, and keep him at home, continued to grow. As Robert recalls these years: "Roger's retardation was a net that restrained and retarded us all."

Soon after the move, Roger left the Queens School and enrolled in a public school program for slow learners. Here he received remedial instruction in reading in addition to the regular classroom activities; he also received tutoring in French, so that he would have something to show off to the other kids, something he knew that they didn't. Interestingly, he would rarely stutter in French, likely because there was so much less pressure upon him to perform well in that language, compared with the expectations he held for himself in English.

Four years later, the family moved again, this time to upper Manhattan. Roger had just been tested again, and his intelligence quotient was reported as 58, down from 75 earlier. That year, Roger had one of the highlight experiences of his life: he went to summer camp in New Hampshire. Tall now at twelve, he excelled in the sports activities, especially horseback riding, competing with and defeating normal children his age. He also worked on his diction and on reading and other academic skills. But it was with horses that he shined, that summer and the next two summers, enough to prompt questions from his parents about whether Roger could make a living some day working on a farm or a ranch.

Returning in the fall, he again took classes in Manhattan, walking to school each day from the apartment on Riverside Drive. He was becoming more independent, encouraged no doubt by his successes at camp. The more freedom he was allowed, the more decisions he made on his own, the more he grew. Seeing this, his parents gave him even greater latitude, although always fearful that Roger's trusting nature would open him to harm or attack. Again, in hindsight, one can question whether the parents were right to permit Roger so much freedom and discretion. There is, of course, the problem of protecting him. Yet, over the long run, Roger needed the chance to succeed or fail on his own if he was to continue to develop into an independent citizen.

The never-ending pressure on himself left its mark on Roger; his tendencies to withdraw into his own room, telling himself stories, soon increased. Equally poignant were the effects upon the parents. Roslyn, in particular, began drinking much more and taking pills with increased regularity, seeking in drugs an escape from the pressures she found in her life. The effects upon Roger's father can be seen in his looking always for some position that would enable him to make "some equity" and thus resolve the problem he didn't know how else to approach. He saw making money to support Roger and the family as his responsibility, and he tried to meet it.

Gradually, things began to work out. Robert T. was hired to work for a Los Angeles advertising agency holding accounts with large drugstores. Roslyn became a division manager at I. Magnin's branch offices, also in Los Angeles. And Roger enjoyed the safety and relative freedom of Los Angeles as compared to New York, blossoming more each month and becoming increasingly independent.

Robert T. Meyers's approach to the problems of his younger son was not unusual. The father is usually much slower than the mother to acknowledge that a child has a problem; hearing about incidents in the evening, rather than experiencing them in all their intensity during the day, probably has a lot to do with it. The father can more easily dismiss episodes as atypical, one-time events that mean little, while the mother finds herself unable to forget these incidents. And, too, the effects of disability in a family on the siblings of the disabled member often are overlooked: there is a strong tendency to expect the nondisabled member to become a third parent, a feeling that since "nothing's wrong with you," the nondisabled child should sacrifice his or her own needs "for the sake of the family." On the one hand, this is obviously harmful to him; more than one sibling of a disabled person has told me of his or her regret about "not having had a childhood." To some extent, however, it can be beneficial.

Robert Meyers was forced to mature at an earlier age than many of his peers, because of his responsibilities to his brother

and to his parents. For many modern-day parents, such responsibilities are duties they would not even think of burdening
a child with, yet a little perspective suggests that throughout
history such roles normally were played by children. One need
recall only the frontier families in America, or the farm families
of the early twentieth century, for examples. Children were
valued in those times precisely because of the roles they played
in the family. And it may not be entirely coincidental that
many of the problems of adolescence in our time accompany
the growing sense among teen-agers today of uselessness, that
they have nothing to do. That was not a problem young Robert,
at least, had to face.

By this point, in 1964, the family began to realize that time
was running out. Robert T. Meyers was fifty-four, his dream
of equity still unrealized; Roslyn Meyers was forty-five. And
Roger was sixteen, almost finished with formal public education. Both Robert and Roslyn were working full-time, and their
older son, twenty-one, was attending school full-time. Roger,
accordingly, was often alone, still needing attention and help
but facing two tired parents and a busy older brother less and
less able to give him the assistance he needed.

So his parents arranged to place Roger in a residential facility
for retarded individuals, south of Los Angeles. Residential
placement for Roger was, they believed, "best for him." With
the exception of three summers at camp, Roger had never
lived apart from his family in sixteen years. He soon ran away,
largely because he disliked the constant teasing of the juvenile-
delinquent residents who lived there with the retarded individuals, and shortly thereafter left permanently to rejoin his family.

Four years later, in 1968, Roger began doing some work
in a sheltered workshop designed for persons with cerebral
palsy, earning fifty cents an hour stuffing parts into plastic bags.
Equally important for Roger, he worked Saturdays at the local
Y.M.C.A., making change for swimmers who wanted to buy

soft drinks. As Robert shows, the work gave Roger an opportunity to talk with nondisabled persons, to feel less lonely, and to do something he considered worthwhile with his time. One person he met was an eleven-year-old girl to whom he took a liking. On January 24, 1968, he sent her a Valentine's Day card. Shortly thereafter, someone else sent her an obscene letter. That letter brought the police to interview Roger, frightening him and his family deeply.

An agent from the Federal Bureau of Investigation, oblivious to the fact that Roger's card was painstakingly printed in block letters and the obscene letter was written in script, focused upon Roger as a likely perpetrator because of his retardation. Writing about the incident with evident anger, Robert points out that early in the twentieth century the belief became widespread in America that retarded individuals were sexual maniacs. Such fears led to widespread sterilization, without permission, of retarded individuals, segregation by sex in institutions, and prohibitions against marriage. These beliefs died hard, and their effects continued to be felt in the 1960s and 1970s. One such effect was the belief by the FBI official investigating the case that Roger must be guilty; it was later found that the obscene letter was written by a classmate of the girl's in junior high school.

The family still shudders at the memory of Roger's close call with the law, not only because it frightened Roger as nothing else had for years but also because, as a retarded first offender, he was subject to penalties much more severe than those faced by a non-retarded individual. Most people would be fined. Roger could have been institutionalized for "evaluation" and "treatment" that might have lasted the balance of his life.

Soon thereafter, Roger shifted to a different sheltered workshop, and then to a third, traveling by bus, his earnings now more than one dollar an hour. Sheltered workshops were not then as controversial as they are today. The businesses operate

on the basis of contracts with larger, well-established compa-
nies, and provide simple, routine work for persons too severely
disabled to work competitively. The Fair Labor Standards Act
permits the workshops to pay as little as half the minimum
wage to disabled employees. Investigations by the Department
of Labor and others have indicated that in many instances
these employees are not in fact provided with training, which
is an ostensible purpose for the workshops, but rather serve
as workers helping the operation make money. Referral from
sheltered to competitive employment is rare; the kinds of work
done in the workshops seldom prepare people for regular employment elsewhere. Roger understood much of this, and found
the work frustrating and boring as well as of little value to
him in his long-range plans.

To cope with his frustrations at the workshop, at home, and
in his daily activities, Roger turned more and more to writing
poetry. Robert Meyers has written that "poetry was his safety
valve, for his frustrations at not having a normal life, not having
a girlfriend, and not having any friends."

Then, in 1969, he learned he was retarded. As he told Robert:
" 'Dr. Richard Koch said I was retarded. I thought classes for
exceptional children were what everybody went to. I didn't
know there was anything different about me or the other kids
at school. . . . But that's why I work so hard to learn the things
I don't know and so become not retarded.' " Virginia, too, remembers being shocked when she learned, as a teen-ager, that
she was retarded. Roger and Virginia had known that they
were slower than many others; they knew that much, but it
was a big step from that to the realization that they were,
and likely always would be, retarded. That's why the shock
was so great. That comes as something of a surprise to many
people, who suppose that retarded individuals do not know
they are retarded, or that they have few or no feelings about
it. For most individuals who are retarded, particularly those
who are borderline normal or mildly retarded, retardation is

something they do come to realize they have and about which they do hold strong feelings. Roger's, quite simply, was rejection: he wanted to pull himself out of retardation.

One year later, in 1970, his parents finally found a facility about which they felt comfortable, a clean, safe program in which they believed they could place Roger. The Home of the Guiding Hands was his home for the next six years. It was there that he met Virginia Rae Hensler, who had also been retarded from birth. Their courtship began simply, as Roger admired a papier-mâché rabbit Virginia had made. "We met at the bunny rabbit," Roger liked to tell friends much later, after they were married in 1977. Short talks led to longer ones, meals together, and long strolls. They were not permitted privacy, however, having to leave the room door open when they were together. Roger, first, and then Virginia, felt this was unacceptable, and they secretly began planning to marry.

Predictably, parental concern on both sides led to long talks with the prospective bride and groom. Agreement, not legally needed, was reached shortly after both consented to take appropriate steps to practice contraception. It was a difficult and emotional decision, because both desired children, but firsthand exposure to the realities of raising children caused them to accept reluctantly that they would be better off not attempting so difficult a task on top of the other demands of independent living and marriage.

During the months prior to the wedding, something else happened to the Meyerses. Roger's father entered semi-retirement and began to take over more of the family responsibilities Roslyn had shouldered for so many years. It was his father who would visit Roger at the facility several times each month, and his father who would tend to the numerous small crises of food, dress, and books for Roger. Using his advertising skills, he plunged into parent groups and other activities for retarded individuals, writing promotional literature and planning fundraising events. And each time he visited Roger, he was impressed once again by how few other parents made even a minimal effort. " 'They were lonely,' he told his older son. 'Some of the kids hadn't seen their families in years. Some of the adults had never had a visitor. Can you imagine that? I didn't want Roger to feel he'd been rejected.' "

Roger soon moved out of the facility under the program's transitional living effort, which provided support services for residents trying to establish their own independent apartments in the community. Counselors took him into town, to the local park, to shopping centers, to bowling alleys, helping him learn his way around and how to use the area's public transportation system. He learned to manage his money, most of which came from Supplemental Security Income, to make the few dollars stretch to meet his many needs. It was an intensive educational project for Roger to undertake, but an exciting one: he had big plans in mind.

His family and counselors were once again impressed by how rapidly he developed under this new program of exposure to life outside the facility. Within limits, and with appropriate guidance, Roger was inspired, by stimulation in the community, to potential he did not know he had. He grew by leaps and bounds. And as he did, his impatience to bring Virginia to join him increased as well.

While he was still at the facility, preparing to move into his own apartment, he realized part of a long-held, cherished dream: to teach. For Roger, being a teacher almost defines his goal, because a teacher cannot be retarded. He would work endless hours at the facility as a teacher's aide, helping more limited residents to learn writing and other academic skills Roger had learned over so many years of intense effort. Even today, he will talk about these "students" with a teacher's fond recollection, remembering how he helped one autistic child climb partially out of her shell and another resident to print his name.

Just how much he was growing became evident one day

when he demanded a raise. As a teacher's aide, he told the program's administrators, he was performing valuable work, worth certainly more than the fifty cents a day he was earning. When they refused to give him a raise, he quit. That act—leaving something he valued so much—illustrates that he was coming to realize that his time and talents were valuable, just as were others', and that he had a well-defined sense of self-worth and dignity. It was not something Roger would have done just a few years earlier. But it is what he would not hesitate to do again today.

Not long after this, Roger announced to his stunned parents that he intended to marry. The response, when it came, was a normal one: wait until you have a job. So Roger, never one to be put off by minor details, applied for and got the job as a busboy at Love's.

And now he was ready. Virginia, who had taken many of the same courses and experienced many of the same activities in the community as Roger, was ready too. The 1977 ceremony uniting the twenty-nine-year-old Roger and the twenty-six-year-old Virginia was the event that triggered Robert's writing, first in the *Post* and then in *Like Normal People,* about the family and the events in Roger's life. As Robert explains in the book, he had been away from Roger for some time and the process of writing the articles and then the book brought him back into the family and its struggles for the first time in several years. The Roger he wrote about was scarcely recognizable as the same Roger he had grown up with, so much had Roger matured and grown. "Getting married," said Roger, "is like coming out of retardation."

IN THE YEARS since the marriage, both partners have developed further. It is almost as though marriage had helped them in a quantum leap past the artificial barriers of the past and into a much more expanded and enriched life. Bob marvels today at how long his brother can sustain interest in a single topic of conversation, how readily and easily he takes care of the apartment and the needs he and Virginia experience each day. As Robert wrote: "The growth and maturity of Roger and Virginia Meyers since their June 18, 1977, wedding has been phenomenal. Their calmness, seriousness, and sense of self are just stunning."

Like any successfully married couple, the Meyerses help each other. Both tend to have tempers when frustrated, as most of us do, but the knowledge that the other understands helps greatly. Virginia will monitor Roger's speech and he will help her with household appliance breakdowns. Their victory at independent living seems to vindicate the principle of normalization, which came into favor in this country only after Roger was already in his twenties. Again and again in his development over more than three decades, he would spurt ahead when given the chance, the challenge, and the responsibility for himself. The philosophy his parents adopted, as much by instinct as anything else and against all prevailing medical opinion, was, "You can, now try; we'll be here if you need us" as opposed to "You can't, so we'll help you." This seems as responsible as anything for the fact that today Roger is a husband, taxpayer, worker, and citizen in good standing of his community.

It is also probably responsible, at least in part, for the fact that Roger still tries, very hard, to lift himself out of retardation. The effort frustrates and at times enrages him, robbing him of the psychic energy he needs to cope with everyday life. One could say that this struggle to become something he is not is Sisyphean in its futility, because he can go only so far and probably has gone as far as he ever will.

One could say that. But when one knows what Roger has done in three decades of intense effort, when at each stage one could also have said that it was pointless to continue, the fact of the matter becomes clear: yes, one could say that, and one could be wrong.

5

STEPHEN HAWKING

"When is a black hole not black?
When it explodes."

THE IDEAS THAT FILL the days of Cambridge University physicist Stephen Hawking are as far out as his disability is severe. The thirty-nine-year-old, paralyzed from the neck down by a rare disease, focuses his professional attention upon objects that are literally light-years away, if indeed they exist at all. He thinks daily about such chilling events as an end to time and space, such bizarre possibilities as falling into another universe, and matter so dense that even were it as small as a Ping-Pong ball, it would still capture everything that came its way, so powerful is its gravitational pull.

Hawking ponders what the universe was like before the beginning. He wonders what would emerge if a star collapsed and disappeared. And he worries about how to find invisible bodies in the universe.

These and other contradictions Hawking resolves by transcending them in brilliantly evocative theoretical frameworks that have awed even his world-class colleagues in physics. They speak of him without hesitation in the same breath as they speak of Albert Einstein, who is widely credited with giving the world the most elegant explanation of nature ever devised. In fact, Hawking's work is thought to make possible at long last something Einstein himself pursued for thirty futile years: a way to unify the field of physics into one cohesive discipline of study. It should come as little surprise, then, that Hawking is generally regarded as one of the world's greatest living scientists.

He has reached that stature while physically disabled to the point of almost total paralysis by amyotrophic lateral sclerosis (ALS). The disease is progressive: Stephen becomes more disabled each year. It is incurable: there is no known ameliorative, let alone cure. And it is almost always fatal: Stephen has no way of knowing how much longer he will live. When I asked

Rochelle Moss, executive director of the National ALS Foundation, about Stephen's condition, she told me his was unusual
in some respects: "The disease is often fatal within three to
five years, and less frequently within ten or eleven years. It
is not often that a person survives, as Stephen has, for almost
two decades. We still don't understand the disease, know what
causes it or how to cure it, but we do know that it does not
affect a person's mental faculties at all, for some reason."

ALS, also known as Lou Gehrig's disease after the famous
New York Yankee who died from it, struck Stephen during a
trip in the Middle East shortly after he had begun his doctoral
studies at Cambridge University. His physical condition deteriorated rapidly, as he began having difficulty tying shoelaces
and walking. Soon he was unable to do either at all. Gradually,
over several years, the disease stabilized. Today, he moves
around in a motorized wheelchair because his legs will not
support his body and because his arms are not well enough
coordinated to push the wheels of a manual chair. He uses
automatic page-turners when he reads a book, because his fingers are too poorly coordinated to turn them alone. He dictates
papers because he cannot write or type by himself. And he
relies upon others to dress and groom him daily.

What does it do to a young man to see a disease destroy
his body—and know that one day it will take his life? In Stephen's case, an initial depression was inevitable. "I thought
I'd be dead in a few years. There didn't seem any point in
carrying on." But then, as time went on, he discovered that
he was going to live. How long, he didn't know, but too long
to spend in self-pity.

He made several critical decisions at this time. First, he studied with uncharacteristic energy; for the first time in his life,
he really applied himself to his education. Second, he married
Jane Wilde, a resident, as was Stephen, of the London suburb
of St. Albans. Third, he figured he'd better get a job if he

wanted to support a wife, so he started working at the university. And fourth, he finished his long-delayed thesis to become a physicist with full credentials.

ALS, it seems, gave Stephen a reason to live his life completely, intensively, and creatively. As he told one visitor: "I think I'm happier now than I was before it started. Before the disease set on, I was very bored with life. I drank a fair amount, I guess; didn't do any work. It was really a rather pointless existence. When one's expectations are reduced to zero, one really appreciates everything that one does have. But the turning point was my marriage. That made me determined to live. It gave me a reason for continuing on, striving. Without the help Jane has given, I would not have been able to carry on, nor have the will to do so."

For Stephen, his disability, however severe it may be, is a hindrance, an inconvenience, a nuisance to which he devotes as little thought as possible. His colleagues and students regard it likewise; at international scientific gatherings, his motorized wheelchair is surrounded by dozens of physicists eager to catch a few words from him on topics as diverse as quantum mechanics and general relativity; the chair is scarcely noticed.

Whether because of his disease or by nature, Stephen has developed a quick and sharp sense of humor which permeates his writing and his speeches. He has become a master of catch phrases which capture the essence of his ideas, making his theories easier for others to grasp. Yale astrophysicist Douglas Eardly told me about several such occasions. "I remember one talk Stephen gave on the quantum theory of gravity in an international symposium at Waterloo, in Ontario, Canada. He ended his talk with a slide suggesting that we would all fall into a black hole. At another point, he said, 'Watch out for virtual black holes.' Now something that is 'virtual' has disappeared. It's kind of like saying, 'Watch out for the dog' when there is no dog nearby.

"Back in the summer of 1977, Rainer Sachs, of the University of California at Berkeley, asked Stephen how long ago the Big Bang was that started the universe. Stephen, of course, has been studying this very question for years. But he laughed and said that he didn't believe in anything earlier than the start of recorded history."

The ability to laugh is, I believe, central to the ways in which successful disabled persons have coped with their problems. For Stephen, these problems are immense. He is not able to control the fine muscles of his arms and hands more than grossly. While he can pick up a book, he cannot thumb through it for the page he wants without extraordinary effort. Perhaps more important for him in his work, he cannot write or type words or mathematical formulas. These problems have forced him to retain in his mind entire calculations until he has completed the mental processes involved in the computation. His ability to do this with mathematical formulations even his world-class colleagues in physics regard as forbiddingly difficult has been likened to Beethoven composing an entire symphony in his head.

Nor can Stephen move about freely. His condition has so weakened his large as well as small muscles that he spends his entire working day in the motorized wheelchair. To get from one part of the room to another, he adjusts a joy stick on the chair, moving it forward, sideways, and backward as his position requires. The chair cannot be folded, so he is unable to use conventional cars or taxis to move about town. Rather, a large van or truck is required to accommodate the chair. And if he wants to get into a building that is not accessible— that is, which does not have an entrance level with the street— he must resort to assistance from others or entry via a freight elevator.

The problems posed by such limited mobility are pervasive throughout the world. Very few hotels are accessible. When Stephen travels, as he often does to attend scientific gatherings, he must make advance arrangements to ensure that he will have a place to stay and a way to get into the meeting rooms. As a prominent scientist, Stephen can depend upon the conference organizers and upon his colleagues to make such arrangements as are necessary. Still, the presence of so many architectural and transportation barriers does constrict his travel and does limit to some degree the extent to which he can experience many things most people take for granted. His physical limitations also constrain the amount of ordinary, everyday housework he can do in support of his wife and children. Although Jane says she had no illusions about how much help Stephen could be ("I have never known a healthy Stephen"), one senses that Stephen would like to do much more. It is probably one reason he gives everything he can, especially time, to his family, in an effort to make up for those things he cannot give.

Equally important among the restrictions imposed by a disease such as ALS are the psychological problems. People throughout the world tend to regard someone in a wheelchair, particularly someone who is quadriplegic and uses a motorized chair, as a person who "can't"; the reactions often are characterized by sympathy, if not by scorn. It is difficult for someone so disabled to maintain a healthy self-image and some semblance of self-respect when even doormen and cabdrivers do not express respect.

For Stephen, the world seems divided into two kinds of people: those who feel tremendous, even awesome, respect for him and those who do not respect him at all. Stephen seems to have adjusted to these diversities remarkably well. With students and colleagues in physics, as well as others who know him as a world-class scientist, Stephen displays an easy self-acceptance and a ready sense of humor. He has learned not to take himself too seriously. He has also learned, as he has said, how much his life means to him, and has come to live each day intensely and fully, much more so than he did before his illness. With others, people who do not know him or his work, the adjustment to their lack of respect must be difficult. Ironically, the very disability that elicits their disrespect also limits his contact with them, so that he is exposed only occasionally to blatant acts of prejudice.

It is a major credit to the man that he has earned his doctorate and made his professional reputation after becoming disabled, not before. It would have been so easy for him to resign himself to ALS and to give up hope of a rewarding life. That he did not do this, and that he forged ahead to surpass even the most brilliant achievements of able-bodied peers in his field, speaks volumes about the kind of person Stephen is. His disability has strengthened him, concentrated his thinking upon what most matters to him, and renewed his determination to live an active and productive life.

Were it not for the intellectual burden he must carry in doing calculations in his head without relying upon memory aids available to his peers, the field of theoretical physics would seem amenable to someone with the severe physical limitations imposed by ALS. Stephen does his work largely in one place, his office, and with one piece of equipment, his mind. Frequent and extensive moving around is not necessary. Nor must he lift anything heavier than a book or a computer print-out. As a researcher concentrating upon advancing the state of knowledge in his field, he does not have to communicate with others as often or as extensively as do some workers, notably salesmen or public relations specialists. Having said all of this, however, one must recognize how limited these advantages are. Stephen does need to communicate with others on a regular basis and at length; the daily sessions with his peers and students at Cambridge, in which they talk about abstruse theoretical concepts, are demanding exercises in interpersonal communication. He must travel across the globe several times each year in order to attend professional meetings. And he must write extensively in order to express his findings and contribute his product—knowledge—to his field.

Still, there is something peculiarly fitting about his work on black holes. It is difficult to conceive of anything further away from the barriers erected by ALS, both physically and conceptually. We are not even sure black holes exist.

Black holes are, so far, more theoretical concepts than observed reality. Describing the properties they are likely to have is, accordingly, difficult. Stephen has tried to help his readers understand what happens in the area of a black hole by suggesting that a black hole's emissions are totally unpredictable. "It is possible for the black hole to emit a television set or Charles Darwin," he wrote in one paper describing the "Hawking radiation" he discovered. At another point, he remarked that "black holes are white hot."

What are black holes, if indeed they do exist? Hawking and his colleagues describe them as intensely compacted areas collapsed by their own gravity. Their collapse accelerates rapidly to the point that the mass contained in a small area is so powerful that not even light, which travels at 186,000 miles per second, can escape. Time and space come to an end. Hawking has proposed that in some instances, particularly with small black holes, minute particles might escape, but this is to date the only instance in which anyone has shown emission from a black hole to be possible.

"The uncertainty principle implies that 'empty' space is filled with pairs of 'virtual' particles and antiparticles (their opposite twins) which appear to gather at some point in space-time, move apart, and then come together again and annihilate each other," he explains. "They are called virtual because unlike 'real' particles they cannot be observed directly, but their indirect effects have been measured. If a black hole is present, one member of a pair may fall into the hole, leaving the other without a partner with whom to annihilate. The forsaken particle or antiparticle may follow its mate into the black hole, but it may also escape to infinity, where it will appear to be a particle or antiparticle emitted by the black hole. Equivalently, one can think of a member of the pair that fell into the black hole (say, the particle) as an antiparticle traveling backwards in time and coming out of the hole." That would be the Hawking radiation.

If such emission does occur, black holes may not always be black; that is, they might not swallow everything so as to leave observers with no way of knowing that they are there. A black hole that emits something—say, thermal radiation—would be, in Hawking's phrase, "white." Or, as he said in one speech: "When are black holes not black? When they explode." The concept that black holes might emit particles and even explode has dominated physicists' discussions of black holes ever since Stephen first proposed the idea. But it has done more than that: it has suggested that the age-old dream that Einstein pursued for three decades without success might yet be achieved.

Physics is divided conceptually between two predominant ideas. On the one hand, there is Einstein's general relativity theory, which applies to great areas in space. On the other hand, there is quantum mechanics, which describes the behavior of matter on the subatomic scale, in infinitesimally tiny particles. To merge the two into one unified field theory has thus far proven impossible. Stephen has not done it, but he has taken the first step, and that one step has moved the theory of general relativity further than anything done by anyone since Einstein. What Stephen has said is that in black holes, gravitation and quantum mechanics govern the behavior of emitted particles. The concept brings together gravity, quantum theory, and thermodynamics.

Is Hawking the greatest physicist since Einstein? Some experts think so. Others are more skeptical, pointing to the fact that the existence of black holes has not yet been established, let alone their properties. When I asked the question of Yale's Eardly, he told me: "I would say that Stephen is the greatest theoretical physicist working on general relativity. His work is of striking originality. Today, most physicists accept the strong probability that he is right. There is almost universal belief in the existence of black holes. But some—notably the team at Massachusetts Institute of Technology, many astronomers, and some physicists like Philip Morris—have their doubts."

If, as Hawking believes, black holes may explode, this concept may help explain the Big Bang that began the universe. The universe may have begun as an exploding black hole. And it may end as one. Unlike many of his predecessors, Hawking actively contemplates the idea that the universe both had a definite beginning and will have an ending. With Roger Penrose, he proved that the universe must have had a beginning if general relativity is correct. "The evidence strongly suggests the universe had a singular origin about ten thousand million years ago," he writes, immediately posing the question: "What happened before the Big Bang?" Noting that "it was Einstein's great stroke of genius" to realize that space and time could be combined in one conceptual framework and that "in general relativity, unlike earlier theories, space and time are not independent of the matter in the universe," Hawking suggests that "what happened before the Big Bang would have no operational meaning because there would be no way that one could communicate with events before the Big Bang. They would not be part of the observable universe."

The possible end of the universe troubles Hawking more. Noting that general relativity predicts an end, because the expansion of the universe is slowing constantly and eventually will stop and begin to reverse, he says: "This will indeed be an end of time with a vengeance: everything will become extremely hot and will be crushed out of existence. Fortunately, this will not happen for at least twenty thousand million years or so." Alternatively, only parts of the universe may collapse, with the balance continuing on into infinity. A star, for example, may explode, he notes, adding: "But in some cases at least it seems that it will just collapse to a point, a singularity of infinite density. After the star has shrunk below a certain critical radius, its gravitational field will become so strong that it will drag back any further light emitted by the star and prevent it escaping to an outside observer. According to the theory of relativity, nothing can travel faster than light. Thus if light cannot get out, nothing else can either. One has a region of space-time from which it is not possible to escape to infinity. This is called a black hole."

Having touched on the beginning and the end of the universe and tied both to black holes, Hawking goes on to consider the chances of unifying all the laws of physics: "General relativity, as Einstein formulated it, is a purely classical theory, that is, it does not include the uncertainty principle (which holds that one cannot simultaneously know both the position and the velocity of a particle). However, every other physical field that we have detected seems to be governed by quantum principles. It therefore seems necessary for consistency to extend general relativity to quantum theory. Although we have not fully managed to incorporate quantum mechanics into general relativity, we believe that we know how it will affect black holes" because the uncertainty principle applies to these areas. This suggests that quantum mechanics may govern behavior of particles in black holes.

Recalling that Einstein spent much time on the problem of unifying different theories, Hawking states: "He failed for two reasons. Firstly, he did not include quantum mechanics which he distrusted because of its element of randomness." Einstein expressed this aversion in the famous assertion, "God does not play with dice." Hawking disagrees. His work on black holes and thermal emissions leads him to believe that there is in fact chaos in the universe: "God not only plays with dice. He sometimes throws them where they cannot be seen."

Einstein's second problem, Hawking contends, is that "the time was not ripe for a unification because very little was known about the other forces in nature apart from the electromagnetic interaction. However, the . . . years that have elapsed since his death have seen great advances in our knowledge of the other two fundamental interactions, the weak and the strong nuclear forces. We now have a theory that unites the electromagnetic and weak interactions. And we are now beginning to understand how the strong interactions might work and be connected to the weak and electromagnetic forces, though we are still some way from having a proper theory, let alone experimental verification. Still the stage now seems set for attempting a Grand Unification of everything in physics. If and when that is achieved, we will be in a position to answer the question, 'Does Time have a Beginning and an End?' "

STEPHEN W. HAWKING was born January 8, 1942, in Oxford, England, and grew up in the London suburb of St. Albans. He was the oldest of four children whose father was a medical researcher at Oxford's National Institute specializing in tropical diseases. Before Stephen was ten, he had decided to become a scientist because he enjoyed taking things apart. At eleven, he received a scholarship to the prestigious private St. Albans School. Much like the young Einstein, Stephen was an indifferent student, preferring to while away the hours rather than study.

Still, he managed to pass the entrance examination at Oxford at an early age. He became interested there in astronomy but found he had more affinity for theory than for observation. Completing his studies in physics with a "first" (the equivalent of *magna cum laude*), he entered Cambridge University under Dennis Sciama, who had begun a program in general relativity. During his final year, after having contracted ALS, he married Jane Wilde, shortly thereafter finishing his doctoral thesis.

Hawking's work area at Cambridge University's Department of Applied Mathematics and Theoretical Physics is jammed with books, papers, and a range of devices he uses to compensate for his physical difficulties. To help clarify his speech, which has deteriorated since the onset of his disease, he uses a special device consisting of a pair of eyeglasses and a box the size of a package of cigarettes. On the glasses is a sensor that picks up Stephen's voice and converts it into an electronic impulse, which is then amplified and filtered into the box. When I called Donald Selwyn, technical director of the National Institute for Rehabilitation Engineering in New Jersey, which gave Hawking the speech clarifier, Selwyn told me the device can improve Stephen's speech so much that almost all of his words can be understood by persons not familiar with him. The institute has fitted almost 750 people with the $1,000 equipment over the past decade.

Graduate and postdoctoral students do much of the routine calculations for Hawking's papers, grateful for the privilege of working with one of the field's leading figures. Breaking for tea twice a day, the group scribbles equations on blackboards, paper, and even desks. "When we want to save something, we Xerox the desk," quips Hawking. At the end of the day, Hawking retreats to his nearby home and spends the evening with his wife and children. He makes a point of not working during the hours he is with them, trying to be as good a husband and father as he is a physicist.

He has received innumerable awards, including some of the most prestigious honors in science. Just before he got his speech clarifier, he was awarded the Albert Einstein Medal in a ceremony in Bern, Switzerland. Two years earlier, he was the recipient of the infrequently given Albert Einstein Award from the Lewis and Rosa Strauss Memorial Fund in Washington, D.C. That honor is often a contemporary recognition of individuals who later win the Nobel Prize. And in 1974, he was elected to the Royal Society, the youngest man so honored in recent history.

THE WORK he has done has become popularly known during his lifetime. Black holes are the superstars, if you will, of modern-day physics. The one-hundredth anniversary of Einstein's birth focused worldwide attention on the implications of black holes for completing the work Einstein began. A 1979 Walt Disney film by Peter Ellenshaw, the $20 million movie *The Black Hole,* celebrated the awesome mysteries of an end to space and time. Perhaps the very finality represented by a black hole accounts for its mass appeal in this day of horror films and books, but for Stephen and his colleagues the prospect of a unified field theory is what attracts them to black holes.

The highly respected *New York Times* science writer Walter Sullivan calls Hawking's conception of particles emerging from black holes "the most important unifying development since Einstein defined the mass-energy relationship." He goes on to suggest the startling idea that the universe may *now* be a black hole, from which nothing can escape. Speculating further, Sullivan poses the idea that black holes, because they are so incredibly dense and powerful, may even prove to be an energy source for tomorrow's civilizations.

The possible implications of Hawking's work extend even further, to the very question of how much we can ever learn about the universe. What Hawking calls his "principle of ignorance" suggests that at the very heart of the universe, cause and effect may not necessarily apply. If this is true, science may never be able to understand or predict behavior.

In other calculations, Hawking has taken one step further the uncertainty principle of Werner Heisenberg, who said that even in principle one cannot know both the velocity and position of a given particle at the same time. Stephen believes that the laws of physics themselves may be observer-dependent, such that "different observers might even encounter different histories of the universe." The 1977 article in which he and a colleague made this suggestion explains that there might be a number of possible branches of the universe, each with its own characteristics. If even some of this is true, we may never understand the universe in which we live.

In his marvelous history of science, *The Ascent of Man,* Jacob Bronowski described the young Albert Einstein's question at the age of fourteen of what the universe would look like from the point of view of a beam of light. Describing Einstein's achievements, Bronowski suggested that his special gift was "to ask transparent, innocent questions that turn out to have catastrophic answers." That is also the special gift of Stephen Hawking.

6

NANSIE SHARPLESS

"As a professional woman who is deaf,
I represent a study in contrasts."

NANSIE SHARPLESS stood by a counter in her laboratory at Albert Einstein College of Medicine in The Bronx, New York, carefully peeling a defective cap from a test tube containing a small sample of frozen cerebrospinal fluid. Moving deliberately and with precision, she extracted a clear sheet of plastic, wrapped it around the aperture of the tube, and fastened the sheet with a rubber band. She had not noticed me standing in the door to her right. I looked around the room, noticing several prominent signs: "Danger: Radioactive Materials." On the bare yellow walls were numerous cabinets containing bottles of chemicals she used in her investigations. Several large containers bore little more than her name: Sharpless. The small room struck me as very much like Nansie: ordered, neat, and uncluttered, with a minimum of extraneous frills or decorative materials. It was a room designed for efficiency and effectiveness, with everything there for a purpose.

She turned easily, spotting me, and smiled warmly. "The cap was broken," she said simply, and continued with her work. The long white lab coat swinging slowly as she moved, she replaced everything she had picked up and placed the test tube in the freezer. One final look around the room satisfied her, and so she unbuttoned the white coat and motioned me to come with her into her office in the next room.

Unlike her lab, the office featured several items with personal meaning for her, notably pictures of her niece and cat on the bulletin board facing her desk, a few plants in the window, and some notes to herself. Two five-drawer file cabinets were, she said, filled with reports and documents, while throughout the room, in bookcases, on desks and tables, and even on chairs, stood neatly piled stacks of journals and research reports. Noticeably absent were any ostentatious awards or degrees. It was a functional room, designed and furnished to serve its purpose. Gesturing to the stacks of journals, she smilingly observed that her colleagues at Einstein often found her collection more complete than their own and would often come in to locate a particularly obscure journal entry.

A co-worker entered the room to ask her about the adequacy of heat in her office and lab. He spoke naturally but watched her closely to be sure she understood what he was saying. She did. As they talked, I noticed once again how simple and direct she was in everything she did. Her light brown hair, neatly curled, was cut short and combed away from her face: she never had to touch it during the day. She wore a high-necked blouse, a mid-length skirt, and stockings, the impression being one of conservative good taste and function rather than fashion and frills. When she gestured, it was for a reason, and the gesture was completed almost as soon as it was begun.

She turned to face me as her colleague departed. "They're working on the heat," she said, disposing of the distraction. Adjusting her dark-brown-framed glasses, she looked directly at me with inviting brown eyes, signaling that she was at last ready to talk at length without interruption.

Over the next several hours, throughout the morning and into midafternoon, we talked about her work as a biochemist exploring the workings of the brain, about her upbringing in a Quaker family, about her hearing loss and its effect upon her work as an academic researcher, and about her personal life. When I had first encountered her five years earlier at a symposium sponsored by the American Association for the Advancement of Science, she had spoken of her deafness and how she was managing to overcome its effects on her life and her work. We had talked periodically through the years about helping disabled individuals to succeed in higher education and in scientific professions. Yet there was so much to this complex woman that I found myself highly stimulated by our conversation.

I had studied learning and memory processes in my graduate work in psychology but Nansie had gone much further than

I in her understanding of brain mechanisms and I discovered just how little I knew about how the brain works. Nansie's vignettes about her day-to-day frustrations and triumphs at Einstein brought back for me many memories of my four years at New York University. The role of Quakerism in her life stirred even older memories of my undergraduate studies on the historical influences of religion and philosophy: she is one of the few people I have met in recent years whose daily lives are shaped by deeply rooted convictions. And both of us are deaf. Her approach to the disability was both similar to and different from mine, reminding me once again how strikingly diverse the solutions are to the problems posed by disability.

"It's hard to explain what I really do. I'm a biochemist by training, but I've specialized in measuring the amounts of certain chemicals in biological materials, so I sometimes call myself an analytical biochemist. To be more precise, I should say that I am a neurochemist, because for the last dozen years or so I have specialized in measuring neurotransmitters, or the chemical messengers of the brain."

Our brains are made up of an incredibly complex network of billions of tiny nerve cells, or neurons, each with a cell body and several fibers called axons and dendrites through which the cells communicate with each other. An axon coming from one neuron meets the dendrite or cell body of another neuron at a tiny contact point called a synapse. The synapse consists of a narrow gap filled with a watery fluid. When one neuron "talks to" another neuron, it sends a message across the gap at the synapse between them. That's where neurotransmitters, the substances Nansie is studying, come in. Each axon is filled with a cluster of little round sacs or vesicles filled with "sleeping" neurotransmitter molecules. When a nerve is stimulated, an electrical impulse is sent down to the tip of the axon, causing the vesicles to release their neurotransmitter molecules into the fluid in the gap at the synapse.

The molecules swim over to the other side of the gap and

interact with a receptor site to either excite or inhibit the other neuron. The neurotransmitter molecules are then destroyed by enzymes or they are sucked back into the axon terminal and again stored. The whole process takes only a split second. Billions of messages are being sent and received in our brains each moment. To help keep things organized, groups of neurons which work together may make just one kind of neurotransmitter, while other groups make other transmitter molecules. For instance, the neurons which play an important role in the control of voluntary movement contain a neurotransmitter called dopamine. There are two major groups of neurons which contain a neurotransmitter called norepinephrine. One group goes to areas of the brain concerned with alertness and emotion, while the other goes to a part of the brain which controls many functions such as hunger, thirst, blood pressure, and behavior. It is these neurotransmitters, particularly dopamine and norepinephrine and their precursor L-Dopa, that Nansie has been studying.

With as many as 50 billion nerve cells in the brain, and with each one of these having connections via synapses to as many as a thousand other cells, the complexity of neurotransmission becomes apparent. An imbalance, or lack, of a critical neurotransmitter could have dramatic effects upon mental functioning by limiting or halting altogether the transmission of information from one cell to another.

To date, seven chemicals have been definitely identified as neurotransmitters, although several dozen others are suspected of being neurotransmitters or of being capable of modifying the actions of neurotransmitters. Aside from dopamine and norepinephrine, Nansie has studied a third neurotransmitter, serotonin, which is present in neurons which control sleep and wakefulness, as well as in other neurons which affect aggression.

"As a neurochemist, I have been measuring the amounts of some neurotransmitters or their breakdown products in brain tissue or body fluids of patients or laboratory animals.

We hope that eventually improved knowledge of basic bio-
chemical events which occur in the brain will lead to better
diagnosis, better drug treatments, and the ability to prevent
serious brain disorders. Of course, the brain is so fantastically
complex that we are a long way from realizing these goals.
Compared to the mysteries of the human brain, the moon is
simple."

Nansie was immediately at pains to clarify the fact that she
is a scientist who works with animals and occasionally with
body fluids from patients, rather than a physician treating people with brain disorders. She works to advance scientific knowledge, not to treat people who are ill. And she cautioned that
despite the recent spate of popular-press stories about "miracle
cures" involving neurotransmitters, much more must be
learned about neurotransmitters before the promises now being held out to the public will be realized.

I had seen stories in *Reader's Digest,* the Washington *Post,*
and elsewhere in the mass media suggesting that neurotransmitters might be used in treatment for a broad variety of
disorders and disabilities. L-Dopa, the precursor of dopamine,
was said to be possibly the most successful treatment ever identified for Parkinsonism. Nansie conceded that this is true but
cautioned that L-Dopa does not cure Parkinson's disease. It
might help perhaps two-thirds of patients suffering from Parkinsonism but it has unpleasant side effects, including nausea
and abnormal involuntary muscular movements. "The side effects are such that no one not having severe symptoms such
as those associated with Parkinsonism would tolerate them.
For the Parkinson patient, the relief from the trembling, inability to move, and other symptoms is well worth the unpleasant-
ness, but use of L-Dopa to treat the lesser symptoms of aging,
including senility and the inability to move about quickly, remains highly suspect and questionable.

"There are important limits to the degree to which neurotransmitters such as norepinephrine are related to mental dis-

orders, such as depression. The observation that some antidepressant drugs increase brain norepinephrine concentrations, whereas some drugs like reserpine, which deplete brain norepinephrine levels, may precipitate depression, has led to the idea that depression may be associated with decreased norepinephrine levels at functionally important receptor sites in the brain. Further work has revealed that this idea is undoubtedly too simplistic."

I asked her to explain why. "Well, we have found that many of the drugs which alter brain levels of norepinephrine also affect dopamine and serotonin, so the relationship between norepinephrine and mental depression is not quite so clearcut as formerly suspected. Then, of course, it is very difficult to know exactly what chemical events are occurring in the brain of a patient. We can't, after all, take a person's brain out and look at it, so we must rely on indirect measures. Most neurotransmitter metabolites excreted in urine don't have much relationship to the brain. There is one metabolite, or breakdown product, of norepinephrine, however, which is thought to have some relationship to events in the brain. There have been reports that this chemical is excreted in low amounts in urine from patients with depression. But we have found, in agreement with several other laboratories, that not all depressed patients excrete low amounts of this norepinephrine metabolite in their urine. Additionally, others have found that not all antidepressant drugs affect cerebral norepinephrine activity. These observations have led to the idea that there may be subgroups of depressed patients and that low urinary excretion of the metabolite of norepinephrine may predict a favorable response to therapy with those drugs which work via an increase in norepinephrine in the brain. But so many other factors are involved that this has proven to be of little practical value."

What impressed me most during our discussion of her work was her precision and careful enunciation of exactly what she meant to say. Part of this was likely an effect of her deafness: she has relied so much upon reading in thirty-five years of being deaf that her speech has taken on the structure and style of written discourse. Every sentence works just right, despite the fact that many are complex in structure. There are no muddy phrases, no "you know" interruptions. But it is more than her experiences as a deaf person. The desire to be exacting and precise is a trait strongly reinforced by the scientific surroundings she has frequented for most of her career. Clarity of expression is essential for accurate communication of ideas.

Nansie told me a story about her family that illustrates both her scientific and cultural backgrounds. During her childhood in suburban Detroit, the Second World War caused severe shortages of many daily staples, including milk. Her father, a biochemist specializing in nutrition, was studying the effect of different diets on the growth of rats. He was also interested in the soybean as a cheap source of food. He experimented with making palatable soybean milk, for example, and several times brought samples of his creations home for the family to taste. That was an example of what Nansie called "a scientific home." Once he also brought home the rats themselves. Reluctant to throw anything out that might be of value, Nansie's father wondered if his surplus laboratory rats might be used as food. Her mother—like her husband, an individual with a scientist's curiosity and willingness to try new things—cooked and served a meal of plump rats' legs to her children and a carefully selected (and forewarned) group of guests. "Most people would throw up their arms in horror," Nansie told me, "but my parents were both willing to give it a try. That's the kind of people they were, and their intellectual flexibility, sense of humor, and openness to experience had a lot to do with making me the person I am today."

Nansie believes that being raised as a Quaker had a very important influence on formation of her values. Her ancestors were among those who came from England with William Penn and settled in what is now Pennsylvania. All were members of the Religious Society of Friends—or Friends, as Quakers prefer to be called.

"Quakerism is more a way of life than a formal religious doctrine. Friends are expected to think things through and form their own opinions, so they don't always agree, but most Friends believe in simplicity, sincerity, moderation, and a single standard of truth. Opposition to war or coercion and the belief that all persons are equal regardless of differences in income level, race, religion, or national origin are also characteristics of Friends. We see 'that of God' in everyone. Quakers were the first to recognize that slavery was wrong. Many Quakers also have a high regard for education and Friends have built a number of schools and colleges. The majority of these are coeducational, reflecting the traditional view of Friends that men and women are equal. Friends were quietly practicing feminism long before it became a popular cause.

"Long ago, Quakers could be readily distinguished by their plain clothes. Nowadays, differences are more subtle. You'll perhaps notice that my clothes are on the conservative side and not dictated by current fashion. My car is ten years old and it was purchased for its functional characteristics rather than for its outward appearance or value as a status symbol. I am supporting a child in India. Quakerism probably has influenced my leisure time activities. Gambling casinos, discos, singles' bars, and fast cars do not appeal to me. My opinions on alcohol, drug abuse, and smoking are much more profoundly influenced by my Quaker upbringing than by my present scientific knowledge. Many Quakers do not drink or smoke at all. Most of those who do, do so with moderation." She added, with a smile: "Getting intoxicated would be *very* un-Quakerish!"

Her upbringing also affected her response to deafness. Nansie saw education as a means of overcoming the disability. She had always been good in school, earning high marks in the suburban Detroit schools she attended. When she was thirteen, she and her family moved to New City, New York, a small town about thirty-five miles northwest of New York City. A few months after entering the freshman class at Spring Valley High School, Nansie contracted meningitis. The disease claimed her hearing twenty-four hours before she reached the hospital for treatment. From that day in 1946, she has been totally deaf. Yet she does not remember the experience of losing her hearing as particularly traumatic for her. Neither she nor her parents looked upon the disability as something that would stop her from continuing her education. Similarly, she was easily able to give up the violin, with which she had become highly proficient, achieving a position on the All-City String Orchestra when she lived in Michigan. "The violin offered me what I viewed as an extracurricular activity. It was never a central part of my life, so I gave it up without much grief. For me, the important thing was academic learning or curricular work. Besides, I was also proficient in art, so I just transferred my energies to a different hobby."

Nevertheless, she sees deafness as "a terrible nuisance, though not a catastrophe." It interferes with her communication with her peers at scientific meetings and, to a lesser extent, with her colleagues at Einstein. "Interaction with colleagues is a very important part of a scientist's professional life. Almost all exchange of ideas occurs during seminars, group discussions, or at professional meetings. These areas of communication are definitely the most difficult for a deaf person to cope with." Her eyes light up when she talks about a relatively new mode of communication at professional meetings called "poster sessions." She will stand before a large poster displaying the results of her scientific work, answering the questions of peers on a one-to-one basis. "Poster sessions are a real breakthrough for the deaf scientist," she says.

She has coped with deafness by communicating in reading

and writing, and by becoming an expert lip-reader. She has not, however, learned the language of signs, nor has she put a special telephone device in her office. Nansie points out that all of her colleagues have normal hearing and that none knows finger spelling or sign language, so knowledge of signs would help her very little in her day-to-day work at Einstein. "I just wouldn't feel right asking people to learn a special code just to talk to me," she says. As for the telephone, few of her professional colleagues have a teletypewriter device, so she sees no need to keep one in her office. "I do have one at home, though, and it is there that I talk to friends of mine who are deaf and to others who have these devices."

I asked her whether she found discrimination on the basis of disability or on the basis of sex to be more of a problem for her. Nansie's response was emphatic: "Deafness is a much more severe barrier to a professional career than is being a woman. In addition to the real physical barrier of deafness, there are attitudinal barriers which can be devastating. Everything I do is 'wonderful . . . considering. . . .' It is hard to develop mature and responsible habits when nothing is expected of you.

"As for being a woman, I don't believe this has been much of a problem. Of course, my first career, that of medical technology, is one that is traditionally a woman's job. And my second career, that of biochemistry, is the 'feminine' area of chemistry. I suppose, therefore, that being a woman has influenced my career choices. But I am not particularly upset about it."

Today, she lives in an apartment within walking distance of her office and laboratory. The doorbell and telephone in the apartment are wired to lights. She believes that she is continuing to dismantle the social barriers that appeared that Christmas Day in 1946 when meningitis claimed her hearing.

"I have been slowly acquiring a professional image. Deaf people are often treated like children, incapable of responsibility for their own affairs. Women are supposed to be passive, not too competent or independent. I don't fit into any of the neat little career niches that people have been conditioned to expect. It has taken time for people to get used to me. As a professional woman who is deaf, I represent a study in contrasts."

NANSIE SHARPLESS was born October 11, 1932, in West Chester, Pennsylvania, but grew up in Ferndale, a suburb of Detroit, Michigan. Her father, a research biochemist in nutrition, and her mother, a former teacher, were, she remembers, unusually flexible and inquisitive. She and her sister Mary (her brothers George, Jr., and John came much later) were encouraged to develop their own interests and to entertain themselves with useful activities. The family's leisure time activities consisted of visits to art or science museums, trips to the zoo, attending "very selected" movies, and reading, as well as gardening and other home projects.

Her early upbringing was, she remembers, somewhat frugal because her parents had come from poor families, while her early childhood years came during the period of the United States' involvement in World War II, with attendant shortages of food and other materials and services. The shortages were perhaps easier for her family to cope with than for many others because of the strong Quaker tradition of rejecting superfluous and useless things. She does not, however, remember her childhood as a deprived one.

Another family characteristic, one of offering hospitality to those in need, regardless of race or national origin, had a lasting impression on Nansie. Her parents were, she recalls, always taking in people who needed temporary homes. For Nansie and her parents, the experiences of having a Japanese-American woman and her elderly mother live in their house until each found employment, led to a longstanding and deep appreciation of the Japanese people. Much later, after the family had moved to New York, her parents once again took in people from Japan, two young victims of the atomic bombing in Hiroshima. They were guests for a year while they had plastic surgery at Mount Sinai Hospital to repair their scars. Nansie herself has since visited Japan to attend the International Society for Neurochemistry meetings in Tokyo. She took her parents with her—and they stayed in the homes of the Japanese who lived with them. "We were," she says, "royally received. It was one of my most memorable trips."

There were other instances of this acceptance of different people. Nansie remembers that her parents welcomed into their home two women from Poland who had been human guinea pigs of the Nazis in Germany, a man from China, and a boy from Czechoslovakia who needed a home while attending college. She also recalls that her mother helped a young black woman teacher to find an apartment in a town which was at that time hostile to blacks. Her parents' example of insisting upon honoring deep personal beliefs and convictions was, she says, "very influential on me."

Another of her parents' convictions concerned the value of education. As she remembers it: "Other things would be put aside—school came first and all of us were good students. Even my brother George, who had a brain malignancy at nine that made him an invalid, retained the ability to do long division and he is still good at table games that require the ability to reason and to count." This early strong educational background was to serve Nansie well later when she lost her hearing. She remembers that she was never very outgoing, but was active in what she considered meaningful extracurricular activities, including Girl Scouts, school orchestra, and community center activities. She liked English, math, and science best of her subjects in elementary and junior high school, and was good enough at them and at other subjects to rank consistently among the better students in her classes.

Nansie points out that the flexibility, openness to new experience, willingness to try unpopular things in defiance of conventional community beliefs, and ability to withhold judgment pending more information that her parents demonstrated are all important to her today as a scientist. She believes that tl.ɔse experiences as a child have a great deal to do with her delight in traveling and tasting different foods. For instance, the cafeteria at Einstein serves Kosher meals, and Nansie is able to enjoy eating there without any special hang-ups about the differences between Jewish and Quaker food preparation.

In addition to her schoolwork and family activities, Nansie early pursued a number of hobbies and personal interests. She learned to play the piano as well as the violin. She liked to paint, and won a prize in a poster contest sponsored by the American Legion Auxiliary. She still paints. She also learned to sew, and during high school and college she made all her own clothes. Most summers before the war, the family went to Port Huron, where they rented a cottage. During the war, the family stayed home. Nansie worked in her father's large vegetable garden, went on bike trips with her sister, and helped her father with his do-it-yourself projects around the house.

Nansie had just entered Spring Valley High School when, in December of 1946, she experienced the sudden and total loss of hearing due to meningitis. "It took only a few weeks for me to recover and then we had to decide what to do about school. My years of normal hearing had given me a considerable edge over the average deaf student, so I didn't really belong in a school for the deaf. On the other hand, my father couldn't afford a private tutor. The social workers that my parents consulted were apathetic. They implied that it wasn't really necessary for me to go to school at all. At this point, my parents made a very important decision. Following the advice of the Director of the New York League for the Hard-of-Hearing, they decided that I should go right back to my regular high school and continue my education. The only real change they decided on was for me to take lessons in lip-reading. Even with these lessons, I could not lip-read well right away. Fortunately, the teachers wrote extra material on the board and some of my classmates loaned me notes. I was able to keep up quite adequately."

Her junior and senior years were spent at Westtown School, a Quaker boarding school in Pennsylvania. "This school was a godsend for me," she recalls. "We had moved twice, from Michigan to New York and again within New York State, and this plus my hearing loss and a very rural neighborhood had cut me off socially. At boarding school, I lived, worked, and ate with hearing boys and girls. This enforced contact broke the ice and I made friends."

Westtown, in Chester County, about thirty miles from Philadelphia, has been a family tradition. Nansie's father, sister, brother, and other relatives are all graduates of the school. "The reason my parents wanted us to attend Westtown is that we would have contact with people who were practicing traditional Quaker values. The school is college-preparatory. The only unusual course offered was a one-credit course on the history of Quakerism. Also, the school is coeducational. About half the student body was non-Friend. I was the first handicapped student to be admitted to Westtown."

I asked her if there had been any special problems for her at the school. "Well, initially the faculty was reluctant to assume what they considered would be an added responsibility, but after a while they relaxed a bit." She smiled. "As you can imagine, there is normally a lot of chatter between roommates after 'lights out.' My roommate and I were no exception. We just blocked out the transom and used a flashlight so I could see my roommate's face. It gave us a delightful sense of conspiracy to outwit the teachers that way. It was not until years later that I discovered that they had not been fooled. They were, in fact, delighted and even wrote to my parents about it.

"Their first worry in accepting me as a student had not been whether I could keep up academically but whether I would fit in. The flashlight meant I had. The school's second worry was whether I could get out of the dormitory building in case of fire. I recall that we had a tremendous number of fire drills during my first year there. Finally, it dawned on my teachers that my roommate wasn't going to just leave me lying there and run. After that, things went more or less normally.

"In addition to easing the social barrier of my deafness, boarding school had other advantages for me. First, to get home for a weekend or vacation, I had to take two different trains and a bus. In this way, I learned to travel alone. To be certain that I got on the right train, I learned to read the station signs. And to be certain that I got off at the right place, I obtained a timetable and counted the number of stops. The second advantage of boarding school was that it was very much like college. This made the transition to college relatively easy for me."

Her deafness "very definitely" affected her choice of college after Westtown. Believing that handicapped people often are overprotected, she applied only to colleges at least five hundred miles from her home. She also sought a school with a well-established reputation for academic excellence because she expected that her deafness might limit her employment opportunities and believed that graduation from a top college would be an asset. For these and other reasons, she finally settled on Oberlin College, a medium-sized school in Ohio.

At Oberlin, Nansie made no attempt to lip-read her teachers in class nor to follow class discussions. Rather, she asked friends taking the course if she could copy their lecture notes. Nansie depended heavily upon the required and recommended readings for her courses. She asked for, and received, no other special treatment, although she did make common-sense selections among the optional course requirements, taking studio drawing instead of music appreciation to satisfy the fine arts requirement, and studying German, which was taught by reading, instead of French, which was taught through conversation.

It was at Oberlin that she developed an interest in theater. She worked on the scenery, costume, and make-up committees of the Gilbert and Sullivan Players. When she wanted to see a play performed, she would read the script beforehand so that she would be able to follow the action. She found dormitory living a boon to her social life, as it had been at Westtown. "Enforced contact broke the ice," she told me.

Following graduation in 1954, Nansie entered the medical technology program at Henry Ford Hospital in Detroit. In this program, students rotated through the various divisions of the Department of Laboratory Medicine. To obtain a master's degree from Wayne State University, which cooperated with Ford on the program, students wrote an essay and took an oral examination. She experienced no difficulties with this program and received her master's degree in 1956. She remembers her final oral examination vividly.

"It was conducted by a committee of five examiners and a moderator. Four of the examiners were faculty members from whom I had taken courses. The fifth, and the moderator, were strangers from other departments. Each examiner was allowed to question me for ten minutes. Because of my deafness, the examiners wrote their questions down on slips of paper. Then I replied orally. The examiners who knew me came prepared with their questions ready. The first handed me a list of ten questions. He handed a copy of the list to the moderator and kept another for himself.

"Everything proceeded smoothly at first. Then, about halfway down the list I discovered that some of the questions had answers on them. I blurted out: 'Dr. Hartman, these questions have answers on them!' It broke up the meeting. A very red-faced Dr. Hartman discovered that he had given me the list intended for the moderator and mine to him."

Following graduation, she worked for ten years as a medical technologist in the hospital's research laboratories.

"My first job as a medical technologist was in a pharmacology laboratory. In 1956, new analytical techniques became available, and we used these to measure trace amounts of hormones in the body fluids of patients. Two of these hormones were

norepinephrine and adrenaline, both of which are catecholamines secreted by the adrenal gland. We studied the relationship of these catecholamines to hypertension.

"My next job was in an immunochemistry laboratory. Here
we were interested in a patient's resistance to disease. Again,
we used a new technique." In electrophoresis, a drop of plasma,
serum, or cerebrospinal fluid is applied to a wet strip of paper.
When an electric current is passed through the paper, the different proteins in the specimen are separated, and it is possible
to measure the amount of gamma globulin a patient has in
his blood or fluid. She used this technique to help identify
patients who had too little antibody in their bloodstreams and
who were therefore more susceptible than most to disease.

After a decade as a medical technologist, Nansie embarked
upon a major career change by enrolling at Wayne State University for her doctorate in chemistry. I asked her what had
led to her interest in transmitters. "It was really just serendip-
ity. I happened to be in the right place at the right time. Back
in the early 1960s, Dr. Oleh Hornykiewicz, who was then working at the University of Vienna, had discovered that the brains
of patients who had died of Parkinson's disease had almost
no dopamine in the caudate nucleus, the region of the brain
which controls voluntary movement. He guessed correctly that
the deficiency of dopamine was somehow related to the tremor,
muscular rigidity, and inability to coordinate voluntary movements which are characteristic symptoms of Parkinsonism. The
logical next step was to try to replenish the dopamine deficiency to see if the symptoms of Parkinson's disease would
be diminished."

Dopamine was needed by the patients' brains, yet it could
not be administered to the patients because one of the chemical's characteristics is that it cannot cross the natural barrier
between the bloodstream and the brain. How to get dopamine
into the brain to see if it would lessen the disease's symptoms?

The answer was not long in coming. In 1967, the late Dr.

George Cotzias, then with Brookhaven National Laboratory, reported success in oral administration of L-Dopa, the naturally occurring precursor of dopamine. It seemed that L-Dopa could pass from the bloodstream into the brain and be used by the brain to create dopamine. The discovery prompted several medical schools to set up special programs to verify Cotzias's findings. One of these centers was located at Harper Hospital in Detroit, where Dr. Arthur Ericsson was testing L-Dopa in patients with Parkinson's disease. Dr. Daisy McCann, who was Nansie's dissertation adviser at Wayne State, was collaborating with him.

"I had measured catecholamines in urine from patients with high blood pressure during my career as a medical technologist prior to returning to Wayne State for my doctorate. So Daisy thought I would be a good person to measure these neurotransmitters and their breakdown products in cerebrospinal fluid of patients being treated with L-Dopa. We hoped to learn how much of the L-Dopa had managed to reach the brain and be converted to dopamine." Their collaboration led to a series of important scientific papers and to presentations before the American Chemical Society and other scientific groups. It also formed the basis for much of the work she did for her doctoral dissertation, which examined L-Dopa metabolism as reflected in cerebrospinal fluid. She was awarded her Ph.D. in biochemistry, with a distributed minor in chemistry, in 1970.

She continued her work with neurotransmitters in the department of biochemistry of the Mayo Clinic in Rochester, Minnesota, where she conducted studies on the metabolism of L-dopa in cerebrospinal fluid, plasma, and urine of patients, and investigated the long-term effects of L-Dopa treatment in rats and guinea pigs. In 1975, she accepted an appointment as an assistant professor in the department of psychiatry at Albert Einstein College of Medicine in The Bronx. She now directs a small monoamine assay laboratory for the departments of psychiatry and neurology.

The research she is conducting on neurotransmitters is exacting and difficult. Because neurotransmitters act within milliseconds, they are difficult to detect and to observe. Nansie has concentrated on quantitative measurement of neurotransmitters or their breakdown products in brain tissue and body fluids, especially cerebrospinal fluid. She works as a member of a team of researchers; others study behavioral changes in animals, receptor binding in the brain, or adenylate cyclase activity. As the team's analytical chemist, Nansie is particularly interested in advanced techniques for more precise measurement of chemical activity in the brain.

She looks at cerebrospinal fluid as a particularly promising substance with which to study neurotransmitters because this fluid comes into direct contact with brain cells and thus more closely reflects brain activity in live patients than anything else available. Analysis of urine specimines is sometimes helpful, as is study of plasma. In one sense, much of this work is somewhat prosaic, or mundane: Nansie is trying to identify the tools she needs to study neurotransmitters. This focus upon techniques, measurement, and analysis will help her and other researchers identify the sites in the brain at which neurotransmitters act. Eventually, she hopes it will be possible to relate specific neurotransmitter actions directly to behavioral changes which are independently observable.

NANSIE BELIEVES that science as a field of study must open itself more fully to minorities, women, and disabled individuals. She is active as a consultant to the American Association for the Advancement of Science (AAAS) Office of Opportunities in Science, serving as a member of the office's Committee on Opportunities in Science. In addition to her presentation at the winter 1975 AAAS Symposium on Science and the Handicapped, she has served as a member of the AAAS advisory panel of handicapped scientists and is now president-elect of the Foundation for Science and the Handicapped, a nonprofit, nonpolitical organization dedicated to advancing the careers of disabled scientists and to enhancing the awareness of members of the scientific community as a whole to the potential of disabled students and professionals. At a conference sponsored by the American Chemical Society, she helped design guidelines for teaching chemistry to handicapped students. She has organized symposiums at AAAS annual meetings, in which handicapped scientists have discussed their work, their disabilities, or their needs. She has also served as a panelist and resource person at meetings to encourage women to consider scientific careers.

She is particularly proud of her work with the American Association for the Advancement of Science. The association's Project on the Handicapped in Science was begun in 1975 to work toward an improved image of disabled professionals as scientists and to encourage disabled students to explore possible careers in science. Dr. John Gavin, a deaf biologist, first suggested that AAAS become active in this area. Nansie and many other disabled scientists have provided ongoing guidance and support for the association throughout the history of its project.

She has made several presentations at scientific meetings and has collaborated in many others. In addition, she is author or co-author of about forty-three scientific publications. In addition to her work for AAAS, she regularly attends meetings of the Society for Neuroscience. She also maintains membership in numerous other scientific and professional associations.

This forbidding set of professional obligations does not prevent her from leading an active personal life. She attends theatrical or dance performances or visits a museum at least twice a month, often obtaining a script or score beforehand so she will be able to follow what she watches. She maintains contact with her family. Her parents are now living in Pearl River, in Rockland County, northwest of New York City, and she visits them regularly. She notes that both were once very prominent members of their community, her father as a long-time

worker for the Rockland County Historical Society and her
mother as a former PTA President and school council member.
Her brother John, thirteen years younger than Nansie, is a
physician who worked for several years as a physiatrist at the
Sister Kenney Institute in Minnesota. He and his family have
recently moved to Binghamton, New York. Her sister Mary
taught junior high school science for several years before returning to school to obtain a master's degree in geology. She
was married and the mother of two young children, and also
was working as a research assistant at Johns Hopkins University,
when she died following an illness in 1966.

As interesting as she finds her work with neurotransmitters,
Nansie is equally challenged in her efforts to dispel popular
notions about the inability of deaf or other disabled persons
to perform high-level scientific and professional work. She repeatedly comes back to the central problem of attitudes. Her
remarks before a student audience at Columbia University are
typical: "I believe that most of the problems are attitudinal.
I am shunted to a more sheltered position. I am not pushed
to compete. I do present my research in public, but I am not
encouraged to do that. I am not encouraged to learn how to
do grant writing or anything like that. I am more or less told
that I am better in the laboratory, and somebody else should
do the public relations sort of work. I believe with encouragement I could do much more than I am presently doing."

I asked her about her oral research presentations. How did
she manage them? "I think what I have said is usually understood by the audience, and of course these talks are always
supplemented with illustrations on slides. The major problem
with these presentations is not getting what I have to say to
the audience but getting the questions from the floor to me.
Usually, I have had the assistance of a colleague for this, but
considerable mental dexterity is required since the colleague
seldom is able to relay more than a brief summary of the question. That is why the poster sessions are so good for me. I

meet my peers on a one-to-one basis in front of a poster present-
ing my work. They read the presentation and if they have
questions, I can usually lip-read them or I will ask them to
write on a small pad. It is so much more rewarding than pre-
senting to a room full of people."

I asked her one final question: what would she say to other
deaf people interested in following her into a scientific field?

"All I can say is this: if you want it very much, then go
ahead and do it. It is not an impossible goal. Medical technology
is a field well suited for people who are deaf. The job market
is good and security for those who have the requisite training
is excellent. Those who wish to go on for a doctorate in biochemistry should be aware that the market for Ph.D.'s in this
area is not too good. In addition, funds for research are very
tight, so job security for people with academic appointments
leaves something to be desired.

"However, I must admit that I have no regrets. I had to
work very hard to get where I am and I am still working very
hard. I do not work a regular nine-to-five job; like most of
my colleagues, I take a bulging briefcase home with me at
night, and when I leave it is often night. On the other hand,
I am obtaining vast rewards in terms of personal satisfaction
from my work.

"I didn't start out with a definite plan for my life. But I'm
pretty satisfied with what I've done with it so far and I hope
it keeps going forward.

"In fact, I'm quite sure it will."

REFLECTIONS

THE SIX PEOPLE whose profiles appear in this book are remarkably diverse in their personalities, in the ways they approached and rose above their disabilities, in the kinds of life style and employment decisions they made, and in their beliefs and convictions about disability. Eunice Fiorito adopted a tough, no-nonsense, head-on approach to her problems, while Nansie Sharpless took a more accommodating, moderate, and quiet avenue to success. Robert Smithdas has devoted his life to working with people who have his disabilities, while Stephen Hawking rarely even meets people with severe disabilities. Roger Meyers has tried to rise above and out of his disability by sheer will, denying his retardation in every way he can, while Susan Daniels has frankly acknowledged her disability and defied it to come between her and her sexuality.

It may appear to the casual reader that these people have little if anything in common other than the fact that all are disabled. I want to reflect briefly upon these portraits and to show what these people mean to me.

I have written about these six individuals because I can think of no more suitable way to express the ideas and ideals represented by the United Nations International Year of Disabled Persons. During the three years I have been serving as the

United States representative to the United Nations planning committee for the Year, I have been struck repeatedly by the fact that one tragically wrong perception dominates the lives of the world's 500 million disabled citizens.

And that belief is that little, if anything, can be done to help these people; that they are more disabled than able; that they can't.

As a result, the lives of these millions are unnecessarily deprived, difficult, and, often, short.

In Washington, Vienna, Jerusalem, Copenhagen, Cairo, and Paris, among many other world capitals, I have run into this conception of *can't* again and again. How, I asked my colleagues from across the globe, can this pervasive and devastating myth be attacked?

Very early in these meetings, I lost most of what little faith I had in the power of mere words, statistics, and research reports. Rather, I came to believe, the abilities of disabled people had to be dramatized. People must be led to see and to believe that even the most severe and profound physical and mental disabilities are conditions that can be, have been, and are being overcome. And so I chose six people with varying disabilities whose lives seemed to exemplify the simple but remarkable fact that disabled people *can.*

This is an exciting and important idea. Throughout the world, one family in every four is touched by disability: at least one family member is disabled, has friends who are disabled, or works with disabled individuals. In the 153 countries participating in the United Nations, at least three out of every five disabled individuals are not receiving even the most minimal kinds of education, rehabilitation, and other assistance they need to become independent, self-sufficient citizens.

In some parts of the world, the problem is even more severe. Nations that have been at war in the past several decades have unusual numbers of disabled residents, especially veterans; I have seen this in, for example, Israel and Egypt. In other nations, particularly those in the Third World, even the most rudimentary preventive and primary care measures are scarce or nonexistent.

I have learned, too, that many nations are becoming increasingly concerned about the rapidly escalating costs of caring for dependent individuals with disabilities. Nation after nation is paying lifelong medical and subsistence expenses—and no one seems to know how to bring these spiraling costs under control. Experts in England, Bangladesh, and the Soviet Union have pressed this concern with me with particular urgency. For cold economic reasons, then, disability has become a priority problem in many parts of the world.

There is yet another intriguing aspect of disability worldwide: it can serve as an apolitical issue around which international cooperation can be built. My own experience in the Middle East, with Israel and Egypt, illustrates the fact that (to adopt the theme of a project I directed) "helping first in making peace those hurt most in making war" transcends political boundaries and generates remarkably candid and open exchange of information and expertise among nations.

For all these reasons, the fact that life does not end with severe disability is of crucial importance. The notion that appropriate assistance, properly applied in a timely manner, can lift disabled people out of dependency is central. We can move the 300 million people with disabilities of this world who are mired now in dependency into independence. We can bypass disability to develop ability. And we can turn tax users into taxpayers.

When we give people freedom, when we remove the shackles of disability and the chains of suppression, we free the minds of people to soar beyond the narrow confines of human expectations. We, all of us, can do things we thought impossible. Certainly, the people in this book have risen to levels popularly thought to be beyond the reach and even beyond the dreams of persons with their severe limitations. Most of them have surpassed the grasp and reach of so-called normal individuals.

This must be important, for it tells us something deeply hopeful about the human condition. If we believe in ourselves, and if the people around us believe in us, there is in fact very little that is beyond doing. And it tells us, too, that should we ourselves become disabled at some point in our lives, not a probable but a possible event, we can rise above and beyond the condition to resume and even exceed the level of achievement we reached in earlier years.

These six people exemplify all of that for me. And they illustrate something else which I believe is important. Given a supportive environment that encourages them to nourish and develop abilities with which to compensate for the disabilities, disabled children and youth can achieve not only vocational success but psychological adjustment as well. Again and again, disabled adults I have known have pointed to certain rights, principles, and approaches as vital to their struggle to become independent individuals. They stress the centrality of their parents' beliefs and actions as the determining factor in how they came to perceive themselves. Indeed, it is difficult for me to overemphasize the importance with which these rights are viewed by successful disabled adults. They seem to frame a "bill of rights" for the disabled child.

These are basic, fundamental rights, the kind most of us accept as axiomatic. Yet they are so often ignored and violated that they deserve special attention.

The first is the right to be helped to become a fully developed person. A paraplegic researcher who is nationally recognized for his work, popular with and respected by his neighbors for his community-mindedness, and a contented family man attributes his all-around success to his parents' influence: "They never let me feel like an appendage to a wheelchair or a performance machine. I got as much attention and praise for idle conversation, hobbies, socialization, and dating as I did for my progress in therapy and in school." The parallel between his upbringing and that of Susan Daniels and Nansie Sharpless is vivid and sharp. Their parents treated them as people, not just as disabilities that had to be treated and overcome.

A second right is to be granted as much freedom and independence as are other children in the family. This might be called the right to fail. One blind lawyer told me: "My mother let me do everything my brothers did. Sure, she worried, but she believed this was the only way I would learn to be independent and self-reliant." One remembers the tolerance of Eunice Fiorito's parents when she spoke out or got herself into trouble with the nuns at her school. One recalls, too, Roslyn Meyers's determination to let Roger play by himself despite her fears that he would be hurt or mistreated by other children. She knew that overprotection could be as harmful to Roger as its opposite, lax supervision.

A third is the right to have one's abilities, not disabilities, treated as the critical factors for one's success. "My parents told me over and over again to do what I could do well," one disabled adult told me. "They felt that my ability to learn, to think, and to create would be what would make me successful." One thinks immediately of Nansie Sharpless and the way her parents encouraged her intellectual and academic development. To deal with the disability is important, but it is the abilities that will enable the child to become an adult who is employable, productive, and independent.

A fourth is the right to have one's disability perceived as an obstacle to be overcome rather than as a crippling liability. A deaf psychologist emphasized the importance of this right when he said: "My father compared my hearing loss to the extra weight a horse carries in a handicap race. But he always made it clear that I could still win the race." Stephen Hawking's parents, wife, and teachers knew that his disability would make it harder for him, but all were united in the conviction that it was just an obstacle, not a reason to withdraw from his attempts to become a physicist.

A fifth is the right to have unnecessary environmental barriers removed from the home. This right requires some explanation. Basically, the concept is one of environmental control—setting up the house and the family routine so the fewest possible barriers confront the child. With a deaf child, this might mean having all family members sign to each other at home. With a blind child, it might mean ensuring that things are replaced where they were found so the blind child will know where they are; or it may mean using a tape recorder instead of a bulletin board for notices to family members. With a child in a wheelchair, it might mean rearranging furniture and putting ramps at doors. With an emotionally disturbed child, it might mean a constant, dependable routine each day.

Environmental control is enormously important for disabled children and their families. It alleviates the child's daily frustrations, reduces household tension, and increases self-reliance and independence. The parents need not watch the child constantly and repeatedly stifle him with "no." What it does is create an environment in the home where the disability is not a handicap. It allows the parents to treat the disabled child as much as possible like other children.

Susan Daniels's mother was practicing environmental control when she habitually parked her car as close as possible to a store, so Susan would have less distance to travel. Roger's mother and father did it when they provided opportunities for him to attend summer camp, where his disability was less important than it was in school and where his abilities, including physical exercise and riding horses, were more important. For Robert Smithdas, placement at a boarding school, the Perkins Institute, served this purpose because it gave him an environment more suited to his needs than his parents could provide in Pittsburgh.

Psychologists, counselors, teachers, and other experts on the care of disabled children stress repeatedly the need for "acceptance" by parents of the child, the disability, and the child's struggle with the disability. Most parents I have known have tried conscientiously to show their children that they accept them and each of their often small achievements as they are. But these parents ask a good question: "Just what is 'acceptance' and how do we 'show' it?"

The same parents feel torn over the use of punishment. They need it, they say, to keep order in the house and to help the child learn not to hurt himself and others. But feeling that the child faces more than enough rejection in a hostile world, they are often more reluctant to punish a disabled than an able-bodied child. Besides, they point out, punishment seems incompatible with the much vaunted but little understood concept of acceptance.

The problems raised by acceptance and by punishment seem almost universal among parents and teachers of disabled children. Roger Meyers's parents worried about punishing him, and as a result often took out their frustrations on his older brother. Eunice Fiorito's parents rarely disciplined her. Susan Daniels's parents, like Eunice's, had difficulty accepting the disability, and spent several years pursuing faith healers and other miracle cures.

I can illustrate some of these problems, and what I believe is a workable solution, through a conversation I witnessed between a five-year-old paraplegic boy and his mother. It is similar to exchanges Susan remembers from her own childhood. The boy—I'll call him Johnny—refused to use his wheelchair and to leave for school in it. The conversation went as follows:

MOTHER: O.K. Let's get into the chair now.
JOHNNY: No!
MOTHER: You don't want to get into the chair?
JOHNNY: I won't. No more!
MOTHER: You're never going to ride your chair again.

JOHNNY: I hate it!

MOTHER: The chair is heavy and you don't like to push it. You get tired.

JOHNNY: No, it's light. It's small. Pushing it is easy.

MOTHER: But you don't want to ride in it.

JOHNNY: Yeah. You don't have one. Daddy doesn't have one.

MOTHER: You want to be able to walk like mommy and daddy.

JOHNNY: Yeah! I want to walk. I don't want to have to use wheels.

MOTHER: You want your legs to be strong.

JOHNNY: Strong legs. I want strong legs.

MOTHER: But you don't see how riding in your chair will help your legs get strong.

JOHNNY: Yeah. Well, I need it to get to school. In school we do exercises. It's supposed to make my legs strong.

MOTHER: You like the exercises.

JOHNNY: Yeah, they're fun. (Pause) Help me in, mom. I want to go to school.

Notice that Johnny's mother never scolded him, punished him, ordered him, or ridiculed him. She did not argue. Rather, she "fed back" to Johnny what she thought he meant. She guessed wrong once, about the chair being heavy, and he corrected her immediately. What she showed Johnny was that she accepted his feelings as legitimate. What at first seemed like a willful refusal to ride in his chair soon was revealed to be a strong desire to be able to walk. Without his mother's having to tell him, Johnny realized that to learn to walk he would have to do the exercises at school. He literally talked himself into going.

It is in many respects a remarkable conversation. The topic is a delicate one. Johnny obviously has deep feelings about his disability. He is sensitive about having to use a wheelchair, which for him symbolizes his weakness. His refusal to use it might have produced a highly emotional struggle between him and his mother. In fact, that is what often happens.

Consider this hypothetical conversation:

MOTHER: O.K. Let's get into the chair now.
JOHNNY: No!
MOTHER: It's already late. Don't put up a fight.
JOHNNY: I won't.
MOTHER: Yes, you will. Right this minute.
JOHNNY: No! Never, no more!
MOTHER: I'll give you one second to get into this chair.
JOHNNY: I won't! I won't!
MOTHER: I'd hate to have to spank you but it looks like I'll have to.

You see the differences between this conversation and the first one. In the earlier talk, Johnny revealed why he felt as he did. The mother learned something important about his emotions. And Johnny made an important discovery. He realized that exercising would help him learn to walk, while lying at home on the bed would not. It is likely that Johnny would be more cooperative about going to school in his chair after that conversation.

But in the second exchange, none of this happened. Mother has no new information about Johnny's feelings. It appears to her that his behavior represents a willful refusal to obey an order; to him, her reaction to his refusal seems a failure to understand him. Rather than learning something about himself, Johnny learned only that if he did not do as he was told, he would be spanked. And it is probable that this battle would be fought again in the days and weeks to come.

Conversations like these, repeated many hundreds and even thousands of times throughout childhood and adolescence, help shape a child's view of himself and of his disability. The six people in this book were fortunate to have parents who tried to understand without coddling, to support without overwhelming, and to guide without directing. It seems to me important that they shared this kind of upbringing, because it suggests something we may need to know in order to help other people with disabilities, their parents, and their teachers.

Examining further the lives of these six people, we can see that they had to work incredibly hard just to achieve what most people take for granted. No one should have to strive that much for such basic, fundamental needs. We must work together to create a world in which we help people with disabilities get the education they need, find places to live, move around in our communities, secure meaningful and satisfying employment, enjoy social and cultural opportunities, and receive equal pay for equal work.

These six individuals, too, were remarkably lonely for most of their lives. Again, this must not be a correlate of disability. We must teach ourselves, and our children, that people with disabilities are more like us than different from us, that they should be accepted as our peers and welcomed as our friends.

For the many parents, relatives, and close friends of persons with disabilities, what else can be learned from the success of the six people in this book? What does it take to "make it" for someone who is disabled? Based as much on my own experience as a disabled person and on my work with parents and others as on the portraits here, I would suggest that a successful disabled person likely would have the following characteristics:

 * DRIVE. The discipline, sheer hard work, and unremitting determination to succeed that characterize the six people in this book will probably be needed by most people with disabilities who want to be successful in life and in work. This will, unfortunately, continue to hold for years to come because surmounting barriers, whether they relate to physical factors, attitude, transportation, or communication, requires a great deal of effort.

 * SENSE OF HUMOR. I do not know any truly successful disa-

bled individual who has not learned to laugh at himself or herself, at the ignorance of most persons about disabilities, and at the world itself. The struggle to succeed is a long and hard one. Without humor, the very oppression one faces will induce a sense of depression and hasten defeat.

* PATIENCE. For many of the same reasons, one must develop a long-range view of life, accepting what cannot be changed and realizing that what can be altered will not change quickly.

* EDUCATION. This is a *sine qua non*. Schooling may be "special" in the sense that it is offered in settings and with teachers especially prepared for the needs of disabled children with particular conditions, or it may be "regular" in the sense that disabled children are integrated with children who are nondisabled. Other things being equal, which they seldom are, I tend to favor regular over special education because the quality of instruction and the level of competition usually are higher. Regardless of how it is presented, the education offered disabled children must never be less than that given other children.

* REHABILITATION. For many if not most disabled persons, further training, particularly in work-related areas, is necessary. Rehabilitation also includes counseling and provision of therapy and other kinds of assistance.

* SUPPORTIVE PARENTS. For many disabled individuals, particularly those disabled early in life, the attitude and actions of the parents are critical. The parent who does for the child only what the child absolutely cannot do, and who encourages the child to learn to do everything else on his or her own; who provides a sense of security and protection against the harsh outside world; who investigates what is available in the community and brings it to the child or takes the child to it whenever possible; and who knows how to "let go" when the time has come is the parent who will most likely have a successful child.

* CURIOSITY. Disability often means deprivation of an impor-

tant source of information about the world. Deafness, for example, may deny a child any reliable means of communication with other people. A physical disability robs a child of the chance to explore as much and learn about as many things and places as do other children. To go beyond these artificial boundaries requires the will to do so. Usually, this means a healthy sense of curiosity.

* INFORMATION ABOUT DISABILITY. People who are disabled often have difficulty identifying the precise effects of these conditions upon them. For example, I knew very few words as a child, yet it never occurred to me until I was a teenager that my problem was not necessarily a lack of intelligence but rather a lack of input of words through speech. By contrast, understanding the effects of disability enables a person to separate strengths and weaknesses and to know what goals are realistic, now and over the long term.

* ACCESS TO TECHNOLOGY. Devices which can obliterate many of the problems associated with disability are available today, and should be obtained and used. There are machines that read out loud for blind people; devices that enable deaf people to use the telephone; electric and manual wheelchairs, automobile adaptation devices, vans, and other mobility equipment. These save the person incredible amounts of energy and time.

* REALISTIC SENSE OF SELF. People with disabilities frequently have a very difficult time coming to understand themselves, judging themselves against others, and developing a sense of self-worth. Others may change the rules so that a disabled child will "win" or "succeed" under reduced expectations; alternatively, people can be so hostile and harsh with a disabled person as to devastate the individual's self-concept. To become successful, the individual needs to know what his or her abilities and limits are. Plato's words still apply: know thyself.

* PRACTICAL AND SOCIAL INTELLIGENCE. I am thinking here

not necessarily of the kind of intellectual abilities exemplified by Stephen Hawking but rather the practical capacities demonstrated by all of the people in this book, including Roger Meyers. This kind of intelligence supplies direction to the individual's efforts. Drive without direction is wasted.

* FRIENDLINESS. A disabled person who wants to be successful needs to be open to other people and to exude toward them a sense of interest and welcome. He or she will need friends at many crucial points throughout life; a friendly person will get it, while antagonism combined with severe disability discourages others from being of assistance.

At first glance, this may seem almost a Dale Carnegie course for disabled people. I do not mean it that way. Rather, this brief list of suggestions emerges from countless questions from parents all over the world: what can we do to help our child help himself? There is little someone like myself can say in response, because conditions differ so much between and within nations, but as a minimum, helping the child to develop and nourish these characteristics should go a long way.

But working with individuals in the family is far from enough.

The challenge for us is to prevent disabilities altogether in as many instances as possible. Prevention is so obviously a priority that one cannot help becoming deeply disturbed by the widespread lack of simple and effective practices. Polio, for example, has been effectively eradicated in many parts of the world through widespread vaccination; yet in large segments of the Third World in particular, the disease remains prevalent. Then, too, many other disabilities are preventable through accident control programs, safety equipment, and medical measures. These must be taken as the serious steps they are and put into effect around the world.

We can think of prevention as having several forms. Primary care is one. Here we are talking about good nutrition, adequate heat and cooling equipment, sanitary conditions, and the like.

A striking number of instances of disability emerge precisely because these are lacking. Malnutrition, for example, can cause retardation. In secondary care, we are thinking about immediate medical attention for problems while they are still minor and controllable. Popular and prescribed drugs, properly used, can form one kind of secondary care. Minor ear infections, if left untreated, can result in significant hearing loss, to take just one example of the need for secondary care. In tertiary care, severe medical problems are treated, often in hospital settings. Immediate treatment of automobile-accident injuries, for example, rapidly improves the condition, while delayed or inadequate care can lead to a permanent deterioration in capacity.

An important aspect of prevention is prenatal care for the mother and for the fetus. Especially with high-risk cases, instances in which a child is likely to have problems for genetic or other reasons need to be singled out for special attention. Early detection of any difficulties and follow-up intervention are crucial. The work of the Inter-American Children's Institute over the past ten years in Latin America provides one example of a highly successful approach to this problem.

We seldom think of environmental protection measures as disability-related, but they are. Exposure to industrial products or processes, high noise levels, and similar conditions can and do cause disability. The same biological factors that are so sensitive to asbestos and other environmental conditions are also vulnerable to drug abuse, including nicotine, alcohol, and dangerous drugs; both the user and the unborn child of the user may become disabled. In both sets of conditions, preventive measures, including community education, are essential.

One of the central purposes of preventive measures of all kinds is to keep impairments from becoming disabilities, and these, in turn, from becoming handicaps. This requires a bit of elaboration.

The World Health Organization (WHO), a United Nations—affiliated agency, has developed excellent definitions for these three terms:

An *impairment* is a permanent or transitory psychological, physiological, or anatomical loss or abnormality of structure or function. By itself, it need not affect the person's life. It may involve a missing or defective body part, an amputated limb, paralysis after polio, restricted pulmonary capacity, diabetes, near-sightedness, mental retardation, limited hearing capacity, facial disfigurement, or other abnormal condition, according to the WHO.

A *disability* is a restriction or prevention of the performance of an activity, resulting from an impairment, in the manner or within the range considered normal for a human being. Disabilities as results of impairments may involve difficulties in walking, seeing, speaking, hearing, reading, writing, counting, lifting, or taking an interest in and making contact with one's surroundings. Just as impairments may be permanent or temporary, so disability may last for a short or long time, may be permanent or reversible, may be progressive or regressive, and may vary in its impact from the demands of one situation to another.

By contrast, a *handicap* is a disability that constitutes a disadvantage for a given individual in that it limits or prevents the fulfillment of a role that is normal for that person; what is normal, of course, depends upon age, sex, social and cultural factors. A disability becomes a handicap when it interferes with doing what is expected at a particular time in one's life. Children with disabilities may become handicapped in caring for themselves, engaging in social interactions with other children or adults, communicating their thoughts and concerns, learning in and out of school, and developing a capacity for independent economic activity.

Thus, prevention can be conceptualized as, first, prevention of impairments; once impairments have occurred, stopping them from turning into disabilities; and, failing that, preventing disabilities from becoming handicaps.

Beyond prevention, we must work to enhance the social integration of disabled people into the mainstream of life. This is the "full participation" the United Nations referred to in proclaiming 1981 the International Year of Disabled Persons.

In many parts of the world, and often for religion-associated reasons, children with disabilities are hidden in the homes. The wife of a former president of the United States has spoken of finding an attic room in a house in Georgia in which a disabled person was confined to prevent familial embarrassment. That this happened in the twentieth century in the United States of America is an indication of just how prevalent such hiding of persons with disabilities is.

Social integration involves permitting people with disabilities the same civil and human rights granted to other citizens of a nation. Some of these ideas were discussed in the chapter on Susan Daniels. The right to vote, to petition for redress of grievance, to move about freely, and similar civil liberties should be granted to disabled people wherever they are made available to others.

Then, too, integration encompasses the removal of unnecessary barriers in the community. When steps are used in public buildings, places of employment, and other key facilities, at least one entrance should be level with the ground. Similarly, elevators are needed where stairs or escalators are found. Public transportation should employ lifts or ramps whenever possible.

One of the most basic elements of integration is also one of the most widely and blatantly ignored: integration in housing. People with disabilities, just as other people, should be able to choose where they will live. They must not be forced to reside in dwellings occupied only by others with disabilities or by elderly citizens. In residential buildings, as elsewhere, the communication needs of deaf and blind individuals need to be taken into consideration.

It is quite evident that all of these kinds of steps will cost considerable amounts of money. Upon a bit more reflection, however, it becomes apparent as well that not to take these steps will obligate a nation to support in dependency people with disabilities for the duration of their lives. That would be much more expensive.

There is no alternative.

Unless, that is, one is willing to take the step followed by Nazi Germany in 1933. The Act for the Prevention of Hereditarily Diseased Offspring was enacted that year, and within a short time after its passage more than 100,000 retarded and other disabled individuals were exterminated. The Germany of that period regarded these people as people who *can't*.

SOURCES OF
ADDITIONAL
INFORMATION

Readers of this book may wish to learn more about the specific disabilities discussed here.

* BLINDNESS. I recommend two sources in particular. The American Foundation for the Blind, 15 West 16th Street, New York, New York 10011 is one. The American Council of the Blind, 1211 Connecticut Avenue, N.W., Suite 506, Washington, D.C. 20036 is the other.

* RETARDATION. Again, I suggest two sources. (1) The International League of Societies for the Mentally Handicapped, Rue Fòrestière 12, B-1050, Brussels, Belgium. (2) The National Association for Retarded Citizens, 2709 Avenue E East, Post Office Box 6109, Arlington, Texas 76011.

* POLIO. Two sources. The National Spinal Cord Injury Foundation, 369 Elliot Street, Newton Upper Falls, Massachusetts 02164 is one. And the World Health Organization, 1211 Geneva 27, Switzerland is the other. WHO may also be contacted through its offices in the United Nations Plaza, New York, New York 10017.

* DEAF-BLINDNESS. One source. The Helen Keller National

Center for Deaf-Blind Youths and Adults, 111 Middle Neck Road, Sands Point, New York 11050.

* ALS. One source. The National ALS Foundation, Inc., 185 Madison Avenue, New York, New York 10016.

* DEAFNESS. Two sources. (1) The World Federation of the Deaf, 120, via Gregorio VII, 00165 Rome, Italy. (2) The National Association of the Deaf, 814 Thayer Avenue, Silver Spring, Maryland 20910.

Readers who are interested in the International Year of Disabled Persons may contact three sources in particular.

IYDP Secretariat
Vienna International Centre
P.O. Box 500
A-1400 Vienna, Austria

Federal Interagency Committee on IYDP
Mary E. Switzer Memorial Building
330 C Street, S.W.
Washington, D.C. 20201

U.S. Council for IYDP
1575 I Street, N.W.
Washington, D.C. 20005

BIBLIOGRAPHY

American Association for the Advancement of Science. "Achievement in Science: Nansie S. Sharpless, Ph.D., Research Biochemist." *Access to Science*, Volume 1, Number 3, December 1977.

Association of Women in Science. "Meet a Member." *AWIS Newsletter*, March/April 1979.

Bowe, F. *Handicapping America*. New York: Harper & Row, 1978.

Bowe, F. *Rehabilitating America*. New York: Harper & Row, 1980.

Bronowski, J. *The Ascent of Man*. Boston: Little, Brown, 1974.

Brown, R. "Dr. Nansie Sharpless: Biochemist." *The Deaf American*, March 1976: 3–4.

Daniels, S.; Chipouras, S.; Cornelius, D.; and Makas, E. *Who Cares? A Handbook on Sex Education and Counseling Services for Disabled People*. Washington, D.C.: George Washington University, 1979.

Hawking, S. W. "The Limits of Space and Time." Unpublished, 1979.

Hawking, S. W., and Gibbons, G. W. "Cosmological Event Horizons, Thermodynamics and Particle Creation." *Physics Review*, Volume 15, 1977: 2738–2756.

Hawking, S. W., and Israel, W., eds. *General Relativity: An Einstein Centenary Survey*. Cambridge: Cambridge University Press, 1979.

Meyers, R. *Like Normal People*. New York: McGraw-Hill, 1978. Also published by the New American Library as a Signet paperback in 1980.

O'Toole, T. "Dramatic Strides Being Made in Brain Chemistry." Washington *Post*, January 2, 1980, A1, A16.

Overbye, D. "The Wizard of Time and Space." *Omni*, June 1979: 44–46, 104–197.

Sharpless, N. S. "Effect of L-dopa on Endogenous Histamine Metabolism."

Medical Biology, Volume 53, 1975: 85–92.

Smithdas, R. J. *City of the Heart.* New York: Taplinger, 1966.

Smithdas, R. J. *Life at My Fingertips.* Garden City, New York: Doubleday & Company, 1958.

Sullivan, W. *Black Holes: The Edge of Space, the End of Time.* New York: Anchor Press/Doubleday, 1979.

Wilhelm, J. L. "Stephen Hawking: A Singular Man." *Quest/79,* April 1979.